Better Homes and Gardens®

CHRISTMAS COOKING
FROM THE HEART™

CELEBRATING OUR WORLD
Better Homes and Gardens®
Family Food Collection
Des Moines, Iowa

Our Test Kitchen Promise

This seal assures you that every recipe in *Christmas Cooking from the Heart*™ has been tested in the *Better Homes and Gardens*® Test Kitchen. This means each recipe is practical and reliable, and meets our high standards of taste appeal. We guarantee your satisfaction with this book for as long as you own it.

All of us at *Better Homes and Gardens*® Family Food Collection™ are dedicated to providing you with the information and ideas you need to create delicious foods. For more ideas, visit us at www.bhg.com. We also welcome your comments and suggestions. Write to the editor of *Christmas Cooking from the Heart*™, *Better Homes and Gardens* Family Food Collection™, 1716 Locust Street, Des Moines, IA 50309-3023. Send e-mails to spoon@mdp.com, or call 800/678-2651. *Christmas Cooking from the Heart*™ is available by mail. To order past year's editions, call 888/547-2147.

Better Homes and Gardens® Family Food Collection™

MICHAEL L. MAINE
Director, Editorial Administration

JOY TAYLOR
Executive Editor

BRIDGET SANDQUIST
Art Director

Better Homes and Gardens®

CHRISTMAS COOKING
FROM THE HEART™

JULIA MARTINUSEN
Editor

JILL BUDDEN
Designer

Contributing Writers	AMBER BARZ, WINI MORANVILLE, DAVID WALSH
Contributing Recipe Editor	SHARYL HEIKEN
Contributing Indexer	ELIZABETH WOOLEVER
Contributing Copy Editors	GRETCHEN KAUFFMAN, DAVID WALSH
Contributing Photographers	MIKE DIETER, ROBERT JACOBS, SCOTT LITTLE
Contributing Food Stylists	GLENDA DAWSON, JILL LUST, DIANNA NOLIN, JANET PITTMAN, CHARLES WORTHINGTON
Contributing Prop Stylists	AMBER BARZ, JILL BUDDEN, ANDREA MCGAHUEY

Senior Food Editors	Sandra Mosley, Lois White
Associate Art Director	Deena Zymm
Assistant Art Director	Stephanie Hunter
Administrative Assistants	Tamra McGee, Maria McLeese
Test Kitchen Director	Lynn Blanchard
Test Kitchen Product Supervisor	Jill Moberly

VICE PRESIDENT, PUBLISHING DIRECTOR
WILLIAM R. REED

Consumer Product Associate Marketing Director	Steve Swanson
Business Director	Christy Light
Business Manager	Jie Lin
Production Director	Douglas M. Johnston
Books Production Managers	Pam Kvitne, Marjorie J. Schenkelberg, Rick von Holdt
Assistant to the Publisher	Cheryl Eckert

MEREDITH PUBLISHING GROUP

President	Stephen M. Lacy
President, Magazine Group	Jack Griffin
Executive Vice President, Publishing Group	Jerry Kaplan
Corporate Solutions	Michael Brownstein
Creative Services	Ellen de Lathouder
Manufacturing	Bruce Heston
Consumer Marketing	Karla Jeffries
Finance and Administration	Max Runciman

CHAIRMAN AND CHIEF EXECUTIVE OFFICER
WILLIAM T. KERR

IN MEMORIAM   E.T. MEREDITH III (1933-2003)

Better Homes and Gardens® *Christmas Cooking from the Heart*™ is published by Family Food Collection™, Publishing Group of Meredith Corp., 1716 Locust St., Des Moines, IA 50309-3023.

ISSN: 1540-5478   ISBN: 0-696-21628-0

*The Recipe Center at **www.bhg.com/siprecipe** contains more than 10,000 recipes and tips, all tested in the Better Homes and Gardens*® *Test Kitchen.*

Table of
Contents

Pictured on the front cover:
Hazelnut Torte (recipe, page 94)

Christmas Cooking from the Heart

will have you and your family celebrating the holiday season the way your ancestors once did in the old country. As you'll discover, the internationally inspired recipes in this book are as rich in tradition and lore as they are in flavor. So help yourselves to a serving of our holiday fare this Christmas and savor the season to the fullest! It's easy—because it all comes from the heart.

What started as a humble and secret holy day honored by a few has grown into a glorious and happy holiday marked by many. Christmas has become a time for families and friends to gather and share in the delicacies symbolic of the day. When people began honoring the birth of Christ long ago, celebratory cooking rose to new heights. As time went on, even though folks across Christendom were celebrating the same holiday, rich—and very different traditions—sprang up from country to country. The villagers in each region strove to mark the season in their own way, with their own special foods.

German bakers shaped their Stollen bread to resemble the swaddling cloths of the holy infant. At first, the bread was rough and humble, but it slowly evolved into a rich fruit-and-nut-laden wonder. Greek and Portuguese bakers topped their breads with a cross to symbolize Christ: The Greeks fashioned their cross from dough, but the Portuguese made theirs by slashing the top of their bread.

Spices worked their way into cookies and desserts, honoring the gifts of the Three Wise Men. These prized sweets often were served at Epiphany, otherwise known as the Twelfth Day of Christmas. Since this day commemorates the Three Kings' visit to the holy infant, King cakes, pastries, and breads are all still served as part of Twelfth Night celebrations in many countries.

As time passed, certain saints became significant, and foods were created to honor them. Many of these saints were thought to bring good luck or gifts to families and children. The Dutch welcome St. Nicholas every December 5 with their freshly baked spice

Italian Cherry-Coconut Cake (recipe, page 88) and
Swedish Grandmother's Jelly Cookies (recipe, page 117)

cookies. The Swedish pay tribute to St. Lucia with their saffron-scented buns, served by the eldest daughter on December 13 (also known as St. Lucia's Day). Like St. Lucia, the young women wear a white robe and a crown of light. On New Year's Day, the Greeks honor their

Swedish St. Lucia Buns (recipe, page 73)

generous patron saint with St. Basil's bread, topped with a sesame crown. When serving the bread, Greek cooks reserve one slice for St. Basil, a second for the poor, and a third for the eldest in the family. A coin baked inside promises good fortune for the new year to the lucky finder.

Hiding a coin or a token in food has become a part of the Christmas or New Year custom in many countries, perhaps a holdover from pagan times. The person finding the coin may find himself with good luck, a spouse, or prosperity in the coming year. Instead of a coin, the Danes hide an almond in their rice pudding. The Spanish tuck plastic infants into their King's bread. As with the coin, the finders are blessed with good luck.

Yet it is we who are truly blessed, because many international traditions have made their way to the United States. And as families from different backgrounds intermingle, we are at liberty to mix and match cultural culinary delights, to create something refreshingly new, yet with roots anchored firmly in the past.

There are many ways to celebrate the season, and *Christmas Cooking from the Heart* brings them all together—deliciously blending the Old World with the New. How you fill these special days is your choice. The worldwise ways for honoring the holiday are our gifts to you.

For example, you can start off a cheerful morning with an unforgettable breakfast or brunch (page 60). From pancakes that go puff (instead of pfff) to French toast with a Spanish twist, you'll open eyes wide with pleasure.

Perhaps you prefer the afternoon or evening to celebrate with friends and neighbors. If that's the case, you'll love our international tasting table (page 40). It's brimming with bite-size nibbles from countries that specialize in appetizers—from Spanish *tapas*, to Russian *zakuski*, to French *hors d'oeuvres*. Just be sure to toast the occasion. Cheers!

And what Christmas would be complete without a grand feast, whether you celebrate in early December as the Dutch prefer, on Christmas Eve like the Scandinavians, or on Christmas Day as in Greece? Our lineup of holiday menus (page 8) takes you country by country on a culinary Christmas tour.

Just be sure everyone saves room for desserts that are out of this world (page 86). You can serve up slices of espresso-splashed Tiramisu Cheesecake or brandy-laced Mincemeat Tart. Or hide an almond in our creamy Danish Cardamom Rice Pudding.

From the Old World comes a baker's delight— golden breads and buttery cookies. Our breads (page 70) are shaped into traditional rings, swirls, braids, twists, rounds, and buns that may be studded or filled with precious fruits and nuts. The cookies are perfect for swapping at a cookie exchange (page 112). However, the biggest cookie of all is a gingerbread cottage, decorated in happily-ever-after storybook style (page 150).

Greek Salad and Golden Roast Turkey with Lemon-Nut Rice Stuffing (recipes, page 26)

Danish Cardamom Rice Pudding (recipe, page 106)

In this season of giving, some of the most treasured gifts come from your heart and your kitchen (page 132). You'll find such old-world presents as Marzipan and Lemon-Honey Jelly to share with loved ones near and far.

The season includes New Year's Eve to be sure, and what better way to ring out the old than with our good luck dishes from across the globe (page 142)? Whether you choose Black Bun from Scotland or Kings's Almond Pastry Tart from France, you'll consider yourself fortunate when you taste the recipes found here.

So go ahead and enjoy the season. No matter which recipes you choose from this book, the holidays are sure to be special because your Christmas cooking not only comes from your heart, but from around the world, too.

Danish Roast Pork Dinner
(recipes, pages 16 and 17)

Grand Christmas Feasts

CHRISTMAS EVE and Christmas Day culminate in heartwarming family feasts the world over. Mothers and grandmothers prepare their special once-a-year meals. From border to border, the theme remains the same, but the foods and their customs vary. The Dutch sit down to a cozy St. Nicholas supper in early December. The Scandinavians and Italians turn Christmas Eve into the main event, before or after Midnight Mass. Others make Christmas Day dinner the feast to remember. This year, why not cook a holiday meal that's steeped in tradition for your family, following our old-world menus and recipes?

Golden Roast Turkey

Prep: 15 minutes   Roast: 3 hours
Stand: 15 minutes

  1   **8- to 12-pound turkey**
Salt (optional)
  1   **recipe Sage and Onion Stuffing**
        (opposite) (optional)
Cooking oil
Kumquats, small pears, and/or crabapples
        (optional)
Fresh sage leaves and/or bay leaves (optional)

1. Preheat oven to 325°F. Remove giblets; save for another use. Rinse turkey; pat dry with paper towels. If desired, season body cavity with salt.

2. Spoon stuffing loosely into neck and body cavities. (Spoon any remaining stuffng into a greased 1-quart casserole; cover and chill.) Pull neck skin to back; fasten with a skewer. Tuck drumstick ends under band of skin across tail or tie drumsticks to tail. Twist wing tips under back.

3. Place turkey, breast side up, on a rack in a shallow roasting pan. Brush with oil. Insert an oven-going meat thermometer into center of an inside thigh muscle, making sure the bulb does not touch bone. Cover loosely with foil.

4. Roast for 3 to 3¾ hours. During the last 30 to 45 minutes, remove foil. Cut band of skin so thighs cook evenly. Add reserved stuffing. Roast until meat is 180°F and center of stuffing is 165°F. (The turkey juices should run clear and drumsticks should move easily in sockets.)

5. Remove turkey from oven. Cover; let stand for 15 minutes before carving. If desired, garnish with fruit and leaves. Makes 8 to 12 servings.

Golden Roast Turkey
with Sage and Onion Stuffing, and
Honey-Glazed Carrots and Parsnips

Turkey Gravy
Start to finish: 15 minutes

> **Pan drippings from Golden Roast Turkey (opposite)**
> **Chicken broth**
> ¼ **cup all-purpose flour**
> **Salt (optional)**
> **Ground black pepper (optional)**

1. Transfer roasted poultry to a platter. Pour pan drippings into a large measuring cup, scraping and adding the crusty browned bits. Skim fat from drippings; reserve ¼ *cup* of the fat.* Measure remaining drippings. Add enough chicken broth to equal *2 cups* total liquid.

2. In a medium saucepan, combine reserved fat and the flour. Gradually stir the dripping mixture into flour mixture. Cook and stir over medium heat until thickened and bubbly. Cook and stir for 1 minute more. If desired, season to taste with salt and pepper. Makes 2 cups.

*Note: If you don't have ¼ cup fat, use ¼ cup melted butter.

Sage and Onion Stuffing
Prep: 30 minutes

> 3 **medium onions, chopped (1½ cups)**
> 1 **stalk celery, finely chopped (½ cup)**
> ½ **cup butter or margarine**
> 2 **tablespoons snipped fresh sage or 2 teaspoons dried sage, crushed**
> ½ **teaspoon salt**
> ⅛ **teaspoon ground black pepper**
> 8 **cups dry bread cubes**
> ¾ **to 1 cup chicken broth or water**

1. In a medium saucepan, cook onion and celery in hot butter until tender. Remove from heat; stir in sage, salt, and pepper.

2. Place bread cubes in a large bowl; add celery mixture. Drizzle with enough of the broth or water to moisten, tossing gently. Use to stuff one 8- to 12-pound turkey.* Makes 10 to 12 servings.

Chestnut Stuffing: Prepare Sage and Onion Stuffing as directed, except add 12 ounces canned unsweetened chestnuts, coarsely chopped. Substitute fresh or dried thyme for the sage.

English Turkey Feast
Christmas Day dinner starts with a bang in England, as diners pop open party crackers and don the paper hats inside.

Sausage Pastry Rolls (recipe, page 45)

Golden Roast Turkey with Sage and Onion Stuffing

Turkey Gravy

Mashed potatoes

Honey-Glazed Carrots and Parsnips

Steamed Plum Pudding (recipe, page 101)

Dry white wine

Hot tea with cream

---

*Note: Place any stuffing that will not fit into the turkey into a greased 1-quart casserole. Cover and chill. Place the casserole in the 325°F oven alongside the turkey for the last 30 to 45 minutes of roasting or until heated through (165°F).

Honey-Glazed Carrots and Parsnips
Start to finish: 25 minutes

> 6 **medium carrots (about 1 pound), cut into 2- or 3-inch-thick pieces**
> 3 **medium parsnips (about 1 pound), cut into 2- or 3-inch-thick pieces**
> 1 **tablespoon butter**
> 3 **tablespoons white balsamic vinegar or white wine vinegar**
> 2 **tablespoons honey**
> ¼ **teaspoon ground nutmeg**

1. In a covered medium saucepan, cook carrots and parsnips in a small amount of boiling salted water for 9 to 10 minutes or until crisp-tender. Drain. Add butter; stir gently until melted.

2. For glaze, in a small bowl, stir together vinegar, honey, and nutmeg. Pour glaze over vegetables in saucepan; toss gently to coat. Cook and stir about 1 minute or until heated through. Makes 8 servings.

British Beef Dinner

After the roast comes out of the oven, British cooks bake the puffed and crispy Yorkshire Puddings.

Cheddar Cheese Wafers (recipe, page 45)

Roast Beef with Horseradish Cream

Yorkshire Puddings

Chutney-Glazed Brussels Sprouts

Mincemeat Tart (recipe, page 100)

Dry red wine

Roast Beef with Horseradish Cream
Prep: 20 minutes Roast: 1¾ hours
Stand: 15 minutes

- 1 teaspoon pink and/or black peppercorns, cracked
- ¾ teaspoon salt
- 1 4- to 6-pound boneless beef ribeye roast
- 1 recipe Horseradish Cream (below)
- 1 recipe Yorkshire Puddings (right)

1. Preheat the oven to 350°F. Sprinkle peppercorns and salt evenly onto roast; rub in. Place roast, fat side up, on a rack in a 15½×10½×2-inch roasting pan. Insert an oven-going meat thermometer into center of roast. Roast, uncovered, until desired doneness, allowing 1¾ to 2 hours for medium-rare doneness (135°F) or 2 to 2½ hours for medium (150°F).

2. Remove roast from oven; reserve the pan drippings for Yorkshire Puddings. Cover with foil; let stand 15 minutes before carving. (The meat's temperature will rise 10°F during standing.)

3. To serve, slice roast. Serve with Horseradish Cream and Yorkshire Puddings. Makes 12 servings.

Horseradish Cream: In a chilled small bowl, beat ½ cup whipping cream with chilled beaters of an electric mixer until soft peaks form (tips curl). Fold in 2 tablespoons cream-style prepared horseradish and ½ teaspoon dry mustard. Cover and chill for up to 24 hours.

Chutney-Glazed Brussels Sprouts
Start to finish: 15 minutes

- 4 10-ounce packages frozen brussels sprouts
- ½ cup mango chutney
- ¼ cup butter
- Salt
- Freshly ground black pepper

1. In a covered 4-quart Dutch oven, cook brussels sprouts according to package directions; remove and drain.

2. In the same Dutch oven, combine chutney and butter; cook and stir over medium-low heat until melted. Add Brussels sprouts to chutney mixture; stir to coat. Season to taste with salt and pepper. Makes 12 servings.

Yorkshire Puddings
Prep: 10 minutes Bake: 40 minutes

- 4 eggs
- 2 cups milk
- 2 cups all-purpose flour
- ½ teaspoon salt
- Pan drippings from Roast Beef with Horseradish Cream (left) or cooking oil

1. If serving with Roast Beef with Horseradish Cream, when roast is done, remove from oven and increase oven temperature to 400°F. Reserve ¼ *cup* of the pan drippings; set aside. Cover roast; let stand while preparing puddings.

2. In a medium bowl, use a rotary beater, wire whisk, or fork to beat eggs and milk. Beat in flour and salt until smooth.

3. Stir 2 *tablespoons* of the pan drippings or cooking oil into the prepared batter. Place ¼ *teaspoon* of the pan drippings or cooking oil in each of 12 popover cups or 6-ounce custard cups. Heat in the oven for 1 minute.

4. Spoon batter into prepared popover cups, filling each cup ½ full. Bake about 40 minutes or until golden and very firm. Immediately after removing from oven, prick each pudding to allow steam to escape. Remove puddings from cups. Serve warm. Makes 12 servings.

Roast Beef with Horseradish Cream,
Chutney-Glazed Brussels Sprouts,
and Yorkshire Puddings

Roast Beef and Yorkshire Pudding have long been served for Sunday dinner in England, usually along with hot English mustard and freshly shredded horseradish. These days, this classic combination also makes a special holiday dinner. Traditionally, the pudding batter bakes around the roast (after draining off most of the fat). Cooks would pop the beef into the oven before church; then the roast would be ready for a noon supper. They might also serve Yorkshire Pudding as dessert, baked with plums inside or topped with brown sugar, butter, or lemon juice.

Dutch Christmas Supper

The Dutch celebrate St. Nicholas Eve with rhymes and gifts, so Christmas dinner is usually a quieter family gathering.

Creamy Meatballs (recipe, page 46)

Ginger Tomato Soup

Spiced Beef Pot Roast

Baked Endive au Gratin

Diamond Raisin Bread (recipe, page 78)

Spiced Cookie Shapes (recipe, page 122)

Coffee

Spiced Beef Pot Roast

Prep: 25 minutes Cook: 1¾ hours

- 1 2½- to 3-pound boneless beef chuck pot roast
- 2 tablespoons cooking oil
- ¼ cup vinegar
- 1 tablespoon packed brown sugar
- 1 teaspoon dry mustard
- 1 teaspoon instant beef bouillon granules
- ½ teaspoon salt
- ½ teaspoon ground allspice
- ¼ teaspoon ground cloves
- 2 bay leaves
- 3 medium onions, sliced into rings
- 2 stalks celery, bias-sliced
- ¼ cup all-purpose flour
   Ground black pepper (optional)
- ¼ teaspoon Kitchen Bouquet® (optional)

1. Trim fat from roast. In a 4- to 6-quart Dutch oven, brown roast on all sides in hot oil. Drain off fat. In a small bowl, combine ¾ cup *water*, vinegar, sugar, mustard, bouillon granules, salt, allspice, cloves, and bay leaves. Pour over roast.

2. Bring to boiling; reduce heat. Cover; simmer for 1¼ hours. Add onion rings and celery. Return to boiling; reduce heat. Cover; simmer for 30 to 45 minutes or until tender, adding water if necessary. Transfer meat, onion rings, and celery to a platter, reserving juices in pan; keep warm.

3. For gravy, measure cooking juices; skim off fat. If necessary, add enough *water* to cooking juices to equal 1½ cups total liquid; return to Dutch oven. In a small bowl, stir ⅔ cup *cold water* into the flour. Stir into juices in Dutch oven. Cook and stir over medium heat until thickened and bubbly. Cook and stir for 1 minute more. Remove bay leaves. If desired, season with pepper; stir in Kitchen Bouquet. Serve gravy with meat and vegetables. Makes 8 to 10 servings.

Oven Directions: Prepare Spiced Beef Pot Roast through step 1. Bake, covered, in a 325°F oven for 1¼ hours. Add onions and celery. Cover and bake for 30 to 45 minutes more or until tender. Prepare gravy in a saucepan as directed in step 3. Serve gravy with meat and vegetables.

Slow Cooker Directions: Trim fat from roast. Place onion rings and celery in a 4- to 5-quart electric slow cooker. Cut roast to fit cooker; place on top of vegetables. Add the vinegar mixture to cooker. Cover and cook on low-heat setting for 10 to 12 hours or on high-heat setting for 5 to 6 hours. Prepare gravy in a saucepan as directed in step 3. Serve gravy with meat and vegetables.

Baked Endive au Gratin

Prep: 10 minutes Bake: 35 minutes

- 8 heads Belgian endive, halved lengthwise (about 1½ pounds)
- 1 medium onion, sliced into rings
- 2 tablespoons butter, melted
- ½ teaspoon salt
- ¾ cup soft bread crumbs (1 slice)
- ½ cup shredded Gouda, Edam, or Swiss cheese (2 ounces)
- 1 tablespoon snipped fresh parsley
- 1 tablespoon butter, melted
- ¼ teaspoon ground nutmeg

1. Preheat oven to 400°F. Arrange endive, cut sides up, and onion rings in a 2-quart au gratin dish or 2-quart rectangular baking dish. Drizzle with the 2 tablespoons melted butter; sprinkle with salt. Bake, covered, for 20 minutes.

2. Meanwhile, in a small bowl, combine crumbs, cheese, parsley, 1 tablespoon butter, and nutmeg; sprinkle onto endive mixture. Bake, uncovered, about 15 minutes or until endive is tender and crumbs are toasted. Makes 8 servings.

Ginger Tomato Soup

The Dutch preference for using spices in unexpected ways dates back to the days of the Dutch East India Company, which began importing spices from all over the world to Holland and Europe in the 1600s. These exotic spices were so expensive that cooks used them only for special occasions, such as St. Nicholas Day and Christmastime.

Ginger Tomato Soup
Start to finish: 45 minutes

  2   medium carrots, finely chopped (1 cup)
  2   stalks celery, finely chopped (1 cup)
  1   large onion, finely chopped
  ¼   cup snipped fresh parsley
  2   tablespoons grated fresh ginger
  1   tablespoon butter
  6   large tomatoes (3 pounds), chopped
      (about 8 cups)
  1   tablespoon sugar
  1½ teaspoons salt
  1   cup half-and-half, light cream, or
      whipping cream
  2   tablespoons all-purpose flour
  2   cups water
  ¼   cup dry sherry
  Slivered fresh ginger (optional)
  Cooking oil (optional)
  ⅓   cup half-and-half, light cream,
      or whipping cream (optional)
  ⅓   cup dairy sour cream (optional)

1. In a 4-quart Dutch oven, cook carrot, celery, onion, parsley, and grated ginger in hot butter over medium heat about 10 minutes or until tender, stirring occasionally.

2. Stir in 6 *cups* of the tomatoes, the sugar, and salt. In a food processor bowl or blender container, process or blend the mixture, *half* at a time, until smooth.

3. In the same Dutch oven, stir the 1 cup half-and-half into flour until smooth. Add puréed tomato mixture, remaining tomatoes, the water, and sherry. Cook and stir until slightly thickened and bubbly. Cook and stir for 1 minute more.

4. If desired, for garnish, in a small skillet, cook slivered ginger in a small amount of cooking oil until golden; set aside. In a small bowl, combine the ⅓ cup half-and-half and the sour cream. Swirl some of the sour cream mixture on top of each serving; top with some of the slivered ginger. Makes 10 first-course servings.

**Currant-Glazed Pork Roast,
Sweet-and-Sour Red Cabbage, and
Caramelized New Potatoes**

Currant-Glazed Pork Roast
Prep: 15 minutes Roast: 2 hours
Stand: 15 minutes

    12   whole cloves
     1   4- to 5-pound boneless pork top loin
         roast (double loin, tied)
    ½   cup red currant jelly
     2   tablespoons dry sherry or orange juice

1. Preheat oven to 325°F. Press whole cloves into roast. Place roast on a rack in a shallow roasting pan. Insert an oven-going meat thermometer into the center of the roast. Roast, uncovered, for 1¾ hours.

2. In a small saucepan, melt jelly; add sherry, stirring until smooth. Brush onto meat. Roast for 15 to 45 minutes more or until 155°F.

3. Remove roast from oven. Cover with foil; let stand for 15 minutes. (The meat's temperature will rise 5°F during standing.) Reheat the remaining currant mixture until bubbly; serve with the meat. Makes 10 to 12 servings.

Meat Gravy
Start to finish: 15 minutes

    Pan drippings from Currant-Glazed Pork
        Roast (above)
    Beef broth
    ¼   cup all-purpose flour
    Salt (optional)
    Ground black pepper (optional)

1. Transfer roasted meat to a platter. Pour pan drippings into a large measuring cup, scraping up and adding any crusty browned bits. Skim fat from drippings; reserve ¼ *cup* fat.* Measure remaining drippings. Add enough broth to equal *2 cups* total liquid.

2. In a medium saucepan, combine reserved fat and flour. Slowly stir in dripping mixture. Cook and stir over medium heat until thickened and bubbly. Cook and stir 1 minute more. If desired, season with salt and pepper. Makes 2 cups.
   *Note: If you don't have ¼ cup fat, use ¼ cup melted butter.

At Christmastime in Denmark food magically keeps reappearing. The night before Christmas Eve, a simple rice pudding is served for dinner, but enough is made to turn it into dessert the next night, embellished with cream, sugar, berries, and one lucky almond. On Chistmas Eve, families sing and dance around the lit tree before sitting down to their roast pork dinner. The leftovers from that dinner become festive rye bread toppers at the special lunch or *frokost* on Christmas Day.

Dilled Cucumber Salad

Pictured on page 9.
Prep: 20 minutes Chill: 4 hours

- ⅓ cup vinegar or lemon juice
- 2 to 3 tablespoons sugar
- ½ teaspoon salt
- ¼ teaspoon celery seeds
- 2 medium cucumbers, halved lengthwise and thinly sliced
- 1 small red onion, thinly sliced (½ cup)
- 4 cups torn mixed salad greens
- 8 ounces thinly sliced, smoked salmon (lox-style) or cut-up pickled herring
- 2 to 3 tablespoons capers, drained
- 2 teaspoons snipped fresh dill or ¼ teaspoon dried dill weed

1. For marinade, in a large glass bowl, combine vinegar, sugar, salt, and celery seeds. Add cucumber and onion; toss gently to coat. Cover; chill for 4 hours to 5 days, stirring occasionally.

2. To serve, divide greens among eight salad plates. Using a slotted spoon, arrange cucumber mixture on salad greens. Arrange salmon or herring alongside cucumber mixture. Top with capers and dill. Makes 8 first-course servings.

Creamy Cucumber Salad: Prepare as directed, except omit vinegar mixture. In a small bowl, stir together ½ cup dairy sour cream or plain yogurt, 1 teaspoon sugar, ½ teaspoon salt, ¼ teaspoon dried dill, and dash ground black pepper; pour over cucumber mixture. Toss to coat. Cover; chill for 2 to 4 hours, stirring often. Makes 8 servings.

Caramelized New Potatoes

Start to finish: 35 minutes

- 2 pounds tiny new potatoes
- ½ cup packed brown sugar
- ⅓ cup butter
- ½ teaspoon salt

1. In a covered large saucepan, cook potatoes in enough boiling salted water to cover for 20 to 25 minutes or until tender. Drain; let cool. Peel potatoes, halving any large potatoes.

2. In a large skillet, combine brown sugar, butter, and salt. Cook and stir over medium heat until butter is melted and mixture is thickened

Danish Roast Pork Dinner

Christmas dinner in Denmark is full of anticipation—who will find the lucky almond in the rice pudding? This traditional menu also is pictured on pages 8 and 9.

Dilled Cucumber Salad

Currant-Glazed Pork Roast

Meat Gravy

Caramelized New Potatoes

Sweet-and-Sour Red Cabbage

Orange-Rye Bread (recipe, page 72)

Cardamom Rice Pudding (recipe, page 106)

Aquavit

Coffee

and bubbly. Reduce heat. Carefully add the potatoes. Stir gently until potatoes are coated and heated through. Makes 8 servings.

Sweet-and-Sour Red Cabbage
Rødkål (RUL-kal)

Start to finish: 40 minutes

- 1 medium head red cabbage, shredded (about 6 cups)
- 3 medium tart cooking apples (such as Granny Smith), cored and cut into ¼-inch-thick slices
- ¼ teaspoon salt
- ⅛ teaspoon ground black pepper
- ¼ cup red wine vinegar
- 3 tablespoons butter
- 2 tablespoons packed brown sugar
- 2 tablespoons red currant jelly

1. In a covered large saucepan, cook cabbage, apples, salt, and pepper in a small amount of boiling water over medium-low heat for 15 to 20 minutes or until apples are tender.

2. Drain cabbage; return to pan. In a bowl, combine vinegar, butter, brown sugar, and jelly; stir into pan. Heat through. Makes 8 servings.

17

German Roast Goose Lunch

The church bells are still peeling when families gather for their special lunch in the land that gave us the Christmas tree.

Roast Goose with Apple Stuffing

Boiled new potatoes

Creamed Kale or
Sweet-and-Sour Red Cabbage (recipe, page 17)

Almond Fruit Bread (recipe, page 79)

Black Forest Chocolate Cake (recipe, page 92)

Riesling white wine

Coffee

Roast Goose with Apple Stuffing
**Prep: 25 minutes Roast: 3¾ hours
Stand: 15 minutes**

- 1   12- to 14-pound domestic goose
- 2   medium apples, peeled and chopped
- 1   large onion, chopped (1 cup)
- 2   tablespoons butter
- 5   cups dry light rye bread cubes
- ½   cup chopped pitted dried plums (prunes) or raisins
- ¼   cup snipped fresh parsley
- ¾   teaspoon ground cinnamon
- ½   teaspoon salt
- ¼   teaspoon ground cloves
- ⅛   teaspoon ground black pepper
- ¾   to 1 cup apple juice or apple cider
- 2   eggs, slightly beaten
- 2¼   cups apple juice or apple cider
- ¼   cup cider vinegar
- 1   cup finely crushed gingersnaps (15)

1. Preheat oven to 400°F. Remove giblets; discard. Rinse goose; pat dry. Pull neck skin to back; fasten with a skewer. Tuck drumstick ends under band of skin across tail or tie drumsticks to tail. Tuck wing tips under back. Prick with a fork.

2. Place goose, breast side up, on a rack in a shallow roasting pan. Insert an oven-going meat thermometer into center of inside thigh muscle, making sure the bulb does not touch bone.

3. Roast, uncovered, for 1¼ hours. Spoon off fat. Cut band of skin or string so thighs cook evenly. Reduce oven temperature to 325°F. Roast for 2½ to 2¾ hours more or until thermometer registers 185°F, spooning off fat every 30 minutes. (The juices should run clear and drumsticks should move easily in sockets when done.)

4. Meanwhile, for stuffing, in a large skillet, cook apple and onion in hot butter about 5 minutes or until tender. In a large bowl, combine apple mixture, bread cubes, dried plums, parsley, cinnamon, salt, cloves, and pepper. Add ¾ to 1 cup apple juice and the eggs; toss gently to coat. Spoon into a 1½-quart greased casserole.

5. Bake stuffing, covered, alongside goose for the last 45 minutes of roasting or until an instant-read thermometer inserted in stuffing registers 165°F. Remove goose and stuffing from oven. Cover goose; let stand 15 minutes before carving.

6. Meanwhile, for sauce, in a medium saucepan, combine the 2¼ cups apple juice and vinegar. Bring to boiling; reduce heat. Stir in gingersnaps. Cook and stir until thickened and smooth. Serve with goose and stuffing. Makes 8 to 10 servings.

Creamed Kale
Start to finish: 50 minutes

- 3   pounds fresh kale or spinach, stems removed
- 1   medium onion, chopped (½ cup)
- ¼   cup butter
- ¼   cup all-purpose flour
- 2   cups milk
- 1   teaspoon salt
- ¼   teaspoon ground nutmeg
- ¼   teaspoon ground black pepper

1. Coarsely chop kale; set aside. For sauce, in a saucepan, cook onion in hot butter until tender. Stir in flour. Add milk all at once; cook and stir until thickened and bubbly. Cook and stir for 1 minute more. Stir in salt, nutmeg, and pepper.

2. Meanwhile, bring an 8-quart Dutch oven of lightly salted water to boiling. Gradually add kale. Cook for 1 to 2 minutes or until tender; drain well. Return kale to Dutch oven.

3. Stir sauce into cooked kale. Heat through. Makes 8 to 10 servings.

Roast Goose with Apple Stuffing
and Creamed Kale

Parmesan-Stuffed Beef Roll,
Cheesy Baked Vegetables (recipe, page 22),
and Tortellini with Mushroom Marinara Sauce

Parmesan-Stuffed Beef Roll
Braciola (brah-zohl)
Prep: 50 minutes Bake: 1½ hours

    2 1- to 1¼-pound beef flank steaks
    ¾ teaspoon ground black pepper
    1 cup seasoned fine dry bread crumbs
    1 cup snipped fresh flat-leaf parsley
    ⅔ cup grated Romano or Parmesan cheese
    4 ounces sliced pancetta or 4 slices
       bacon, chopped
    4 cloves garlic, minced
    2 tablespoons olive oil
    1 28-ounce can whole Italian-style
       tomatoes, undrained and cut up
    1 6-ounce can tomato paste
    ¾ cup water
    3 tablespoons snipped fresh basil or
       1½ teaspoons dried basil, crushed
    Fresh flat-leaf parsley sprigs (optional)

1. Preheat oven to 325°F. Cover each flank steak with plastic wrap. Working from the center to the edges and replacing wrap as needed, pound each steak first with toothed side, then with flat side of a meat mallet to an even thickness, making two 12×9-inch rectangles. Remove wrap. Sprinkle pepper onto steaks; set aside.

2. For filling, in a medium bowl, combine bread crumbs, snipped parsley, cheese, pancetta, and garlic. Sprinkle filling evenly onto steaks. Starting with a short side, roll up each steak into a spiral. Tie rolls in several places with heavy kitchen string.

3. In a large ovenproof skillet or Dutch oven, brown meat rolls on all sides in hot oil. Remove meat rolls; set aside. Pour off drippings.

4. Add tomatoes to pan; stir to loosen browned bits. Stir in tomato paste, water, and basil. Return meat rolls to pan. Cover; bake about 1½ hours or until meat is tender.

5. Remove strings from meat rolls; slice meat. Serve with tomato mixture. If desired, garnish with parsley sprigs. Makes 8 to 10 servings.

Italian Pasta Buffet

In Italy, extended families gather for Christmas dinner before Midnight Mass. Since some Italians prefer not to eat meat on Christmas Eve, a buffet lets everyone choose.

Basil-Pepper Crostini (recipe, page 57)

Minestrone (recipe, page 22)

Tortellini with Mushroom Marinara Sauce

Parmesan-Stuffed Beef Roll

Cheesy Baked Vegetables (recipe, page 22)

Garlic bread

Cherry-Almond Biscotti (recipe, page 131)

Chianti red wine

Tortellini with Mushroom Marinara Sauce
Start to finish: 15 minutes

    2 9-ounce packages refrigerated
       cheese- or meat-filled tortellini
    2 cups sliced fresh crimini or button
       mushrooms
    1 tablespoon snipped fresh oregano or
       1 teaspoon dried oregano, crushed
    2 cloves garlic, minced
    2 tablespoons olive oil
    2 15-ounce cans chunky pasta-style
       tomatoes, undrained
    ¼ cup canned tomato paste
    Finely shredded Parmesan cheese
    Fresh oregano sprigs (optional)

1. Cook tortellini according to package directions. Drain; keep warm.

2. Meanwhile, for sauce, in a large skillet, cook mushrooms, snipped oregano, and garlic in hot oil until mushrooms are tender.

3. Sir in tomatoes and tomato paste. Bring to boiling; reduce heat. Simmer, uncovered, for 2 to 3 minutes or until desired consistency.

4. To serve, spoon sauce over tortellini. Top with Parmesan cheese. If desired, garnish with oregano sprigs. Makes 8 to 10 first-course servings.

Minestrone
Start to finish: 25 minutes

3   14-ounce cans chicken broth
2   14½-ounce cans stewed tomatoes, undrained
1   15-ounce can white kidney beans (cannellini), rinsed and drained
1   15-ounce can chickpeas (garbanzo beans), rinsed and drained
1   6-ounce can tomato paste
2   teaspoons dried Italian seasoning, crushed
2   cups loose-pack frozen mixed vegetables (such as Italian blend)
2   cups fresh spinach leaves, cut into strips
2   cups cooked medium pasta (such as medium shell macaroni or mostaccioli)
Finely shredded Parmesan cheese (optional)

1. In a 4-quart Dutch oven, combine chicken broth, tomatoes, white kidney beans, chickpeas, tomato paste, and Italian seasoning. Bring to boiling; stir in mixed vegetables. Reduce heat. Cover and simmer about 10 minutes or until vegetables are tender.

2. Stir in spinach and cooked pasta; heat through. If desired, sprinkle with Parmesan. Makes 12 first-course or 8 main-dish servings.

Christmas in Italy begins on December 13 (St. Lucia's Day) and lasts though January 6 (Epiphany or Twelfth Night), but it is really Christmas Eve that is the high point. On that night, before or after Mass, extended families gather for a big meal. The "more is merrier" saying applies to both food and the number of people. A focal point in every home is the *presepio* or nativity scene. Before the *cenone* (the great Christmas Eve supper), families gather around their *presepio* to pray and sing carols.

Cheesy Baked Vegetables
Verdure al Forno
(vehr-DOO-reh ahl FOHR-noh)
Pictured on page 20.
Prep: 25 minutes Bake: 40 minutes

1   shallot, chopped
2   tablespoons olive oil
8   ounces fresh mushrooms, halved or quartered
4   medium zucchini, sliced (5 cups)
4   large tomatoes or 8 roma tomatoes, peeled and sliced (3 cups)
3   tablespoons fresh basil, shredded
½   teaspoon salt
¼   teaspoon ground black pepper
2   ounces mozzarella cheese, sliced
½   cup soft bread crumbs
2   tablespoons finely shredded Romano cheese
1   tablespoon butter, melted

1. Preheat oven to 350°F. In a large skillet, cook shallot in hot oil over medium heat for 2 to 3 minutes or until tender. Add mushrooms; cook about 5 minutes more or until tender. Remove skillet from heat.

2. Lightly butter a shallow 2-quart au gratin dish or 2-quart rectangular baking dish. Layer zucchini and tomatoes in prepared dish. Sprinkle tomatoes with basil, salt, and pepper. Layer the mushroom mixture and mozzarella cheese over the tomato layer.

3. In a small bowl, combine bread crumbs, Romano cheese, and melted butter. Sprinkle crumb mixture evenly over layered vegetables.

4. Bake, covered, for 30 minutes. Uncover; bake about 10 minutes or until brown and bubbly. Makes 10 servings.

Fennel and Cauliflower Salad
Prep: 30 minutes Chill: 2 hours

　2　medium fennel bulbs (about 1 pound)
　3　cups cauliflower florets
　⅓　cup olive oil
　⅓　cup white balsamic vinegar or white wine vinegar
　2　tablespoons snipped fresh basil
　1　clove garlic, minced
　½　teaspoon anise seeds
　¼　teaspoon salt
　¼　teaspoon ground black pepper
　4　to 5 cups fresh spinach leaves
　2　medium tomatoes, chopped
　¼　cup finely shredded Parmesan cheese

1. Trim fennel; quarter lengthwise but do not remove core. Place fennel in a microwave-safe casserole. Add 2 tablespoons *water*. Cover and microwave on 100% power (high) for 5 to 7 minutes or until almost tender; drain. Cut into ¼- to ½-inch-thick slices, discarding core.

2. Place cauliflower in a microwave-safe casserole. Add 2 tablespoons *water*. Cover and microwave on 100% power (high) about 4 minutes or until almost tender; drain. Cover; chill fennel and cauliflower for 2 to 24 hours.

3. Meanwhile, for dressing, in a small bowl, whisk together oil, vinegar, basil, garlic, anise seeds, salt, and pepper until smooth; set aside.

4. Arrange the spinach on eight to ten salad plates. Arrange fennel, cauliflower, and tomatoes on spinach. Drizzle with dressing. Top with Parmesan. Makes 8 to 10 first-course servings.

Italian Turkey Dinner

Christmas Day means another big family feast for food-loving Italians, a sit-down dinner with turkey at the center.

Shrimp and Tomato Pizzettas (recipe, page 55)

Fennel and Cauliflower Salad

Golden Roast Turkey with Chestnut Stuffing
(recipes, pages 10 and 11)

Turkey Gravy (recipe, page 11)

Steamed green beans

Anise-Raisin Ring (recipe, page 81)

Tiramisu Cheesecake (recipe, page 89)

Chianti red wine

Espresso

Fennel and Cauliflower Salad

Greek Christmas Eve Supper

Greeks serve Christ's Bread and honey as part of their Christmas Eve supper, as a reminder of Christ's blessings.

Herbed Rice-Stuffed Grape Leaves (recipe, page 53)

Spiced Macaroni and Beef

Dilled Artichokes and Beans
or Yogurt Baked Tomatoes

Christ's Bread (recipe, page 83)

Honey-Walnut Phyllo Pastries (recipe, page 108)

Retsina white wine

Ouzo

Yogurt Baked Tomatoes
Prep: 10 minutes Bake: 25 minutes

    4 large tomatoes, cored and halved
       crosswise
    1 cup plain yogurt
    4 teaspoons all-purpose flour
    1 teaspoon dried marjoram, crushed
  1/3 cup grated Parmesan or Romano
       cheese

1. Preheat oven to 350°F. Place tomato halves, cut sides up, in an ungreased 3-quart rectangular baking dish.

2. In a small bowl, stir together yogurt, flour, and marjoram. Spoon yogurt mixture onto tomato halves. Sprinkle with cheese.

3. Bake, uncovered, about 25 minutes or until tomatoes are heated through. Makes 8 servings.

Spiced Macaroni and Beef
Pastitsio (pah-STEET-see-oh)
Prep: 30 minutes Bake: 40 minutes
Stand: 10 minutes

    1 pound ground lamb or lean ground beef
    1 large onion, chopped (1 cup)
    1 8-ounce can tomato sauce
  1/2 teaspoon ground cinnamon
  1/4 teaspoon salt
  1/4 teaspoon ground nutmeg
    6 ounces dried elbow macaroni (1½ cups)
    2 eggs
 1¾ cups milk
  1/4 cup butter, melted
  2/3 cup shredded kasseri, Romano,
       or Parmesan cheese
    3 tablespoons all-purpose flour

1. Preheat oven to 350°F. For meat sauce, in a large skillet, cook ground meat and onion until meat is brown. Drain off fat. Stir in tomato sauce, cinnamon, salt, and nutmeg. Bring to boiling; reduce heat. Cook and stir just until thickened.

2. Meanwhile, cook macaroni according to package directions. Drain; rinse and drain. In a large bowl, beat *one* of the eggs. Stir in macaroni, *1/4 cup* of the milk, and *2 tablespoons* of the butter. Stir in *1/3 cup* of the cheese. Set aside.

3. For cream sauce, in a small saucepan, melt remaining *2 tablespoons* butter over medium heat. Stir in flour. Gradually add remaining *1½ cups* milk. Cook and stir until thickened and bubbly. In a medium bowl, beat remaining egg; gradually stir in hot mixture. Return to saucepan. Stir in remaining *1/3 cup* cheese. Set aside.

4. Grease a 2-quart square baking dish. Spread *half* of the macaroni mixture in prepared dish. Top with meat sauce and remaining macaroni mixture. Pour cream sauce over all.

5. Bake, uncovered, for 40 to 45 minutes or until heated through (165°F). Let stand for 10 minutes before serving. Makes 6 servings.

Make-Ahead Tip: Prepare Spiced Macaroni and Beef as directed through step 4. Cover and chill up to 4 hours. Bake, uncovered, in a 350°F oven for 45 to 55 minutes or until heated through (165°F). Let stand for 10 minutes before serving.

Dilled Artichokes and Beans
Start to finish: 30 minutes

1¼ **pounds fresh green beans, trimmed and**
    halved, or one 16-ounce package frozen
    whole green beans, halved
 2 **8- to 10-ounce packages frozen**
    artichoke hearts
 2 **tablespoons finely chopped onion**
 1 **clove garlic, minced**
 1 **tablespoon olive oil**
 1 **cup chicken broth**
 ½ **teaspoon finely shredded lemon peel**
 3 **tablespoons lemon juice**
 1 **teaspoons all-purpose flour**
 2 **tablespoons snipped fresh dill or**
    1 teaspoon dried dill weed
 Salt
 Ground black pepper

1. Arrange green beans in a steamer basket; top with artichoke hearts. In a 4-quart Dutch oven, place steamer basket over boiling water. Cover and steam about 15 minutes or until beans are tender. Transfer to a large bowl.

2. Meanwhile, for sauce, in a small saucepan, cook onion and garlic in hot oil until tender. Add broth; bring to boiling. In a small bowl, stir together lemon peel, lemon juice, and flour until smooth; add to broth mixture. Cook and stir until thickened and bubbly; cook and stir for 1 minute more. Remove from heat. Stir in dill.

3. Toss *half* of the sauce with green beans and artichokes. Season to taste with salt and pepper. Arrange on a platter; serve with remaining sauce. Makes 8 to 10 servings.

Dilled Artichokes and Beans

Greek Christmas Day Lunch

Christmas lunch in Greece is a long affair that begins at noon with appetizers and ends after sunset with sweets.

Stuffed Phyllo Triangles (recipe, page 52)

Greek Salad

Golden Roast Turkey (recipe, page 10)
with Lemon-Nut Rice Stuffing

Pita bread

Orange Phyllo Diamonds (recipe, page 109)

Almond Balls (recipe, page 127)

Retsina white wine

Ouzo

Greek Salad
Start to finish: 20 minutes

 6 medium tomatoes, cut into wedges
 2 medium cucumbers, halved lengthwise
    and thinly sliced
 2 small red onions, cut into thin wedges
 1 recipe Greek Vinaigrette (below)
16 to 20 kalamata olives or ripe olives
 4 ounces feta cheese, crumbled
    (1 cup)

1. In a large salad bowl, combine tomato, cucumber, and onion. Pour Greek Vinaigrette over vegetables; toss gently to coat. Sprinkle with olives and cheese. Makes 8 first-course servings.

Greek Vinaigrette: In a screw-top jar, combine ¼ cup olive oil or salad oil, ¼ cup lemon juice, 4 teaspoons snipped fresh oregano or 1 teaspoon crushed dried oregano, ¼ teaspoon salt, and ¼ teaspoon ground black pepper. Cover; shake well.

Lemon-Nut Rice Stuffing
Prep: 40 minutes Bake: 45 minutes

 6 slices bacon
 1 large onion, chopped (1 cup)
 3 cloves garlic, minced
 2 cups long grain rice
 4 cups chicken broth
 2 medium carrots, shredded (1 cup)
 1 tablespoon snipped fresh rosemary or
    oregano or 1 teaspoon dried rosemary
    or oregano, crushed
 ½ teaspoon salt
 ½ teaspoon ground black pepper
 ¼ teaspoon ground nutmeg
 ½ cup snipped fresh parsley
 ½ cup pine nuts or slivered almonds
 2 teaspoons finely shredded lemon peel

1. In a 12-inch skillet, cook bacon until crisp. Drain bacon on paper towels, reserving *2 tablespoons* drippings in skillet.

2. In the same skillet, cook onion and garlic in hot reserved drippings until tender, stirring often. Stir in uncooked rice. Stir in chicken broth, carrot, rosemary, salt, pepper, and nutmeg. Bring to boiling; reduce heat. Cover and simmer for 20 to 25 minutes or until rice is tender and liquid is absorbed.

3. Crumble bacon; stir into rice mixture. Stir in parsley, nuts, and shredded lemon peel. Serve immediately. (Or use to stuff one 8- to 12-pound turkey; place remaining stuffing in a greased casserole. Cover and chill stuffing while turkey roasts. Place the casserole in the 325°F oven alongside the turkey for the last 30 to 45 minutes of roasting or until heated through [165°F].) Makes 10 to 12 servings.

Make-Ahead Tip: Prepare Lemon-Nut Rice Stuffing as directed. Spoon into a greased 2-quart casserole. Cover and chill for 4 to 24 hours. To serve, bake, covered, in a 325°F oven for 45 to 60 minutes or until heated through.

**Greek Salad and
Golden Roast Turkey with
Lemon-Nut Rice Stuffing**

Christmas Eve and Day in Greece are observed with less fanfare than other religious holidays. For example, no presents are exchanged (that is done on New Year's or St. Basil's Day). For many Greeks, Christmas Eve is a day of fasting or abstaining from meat. Christmas itself is traditionally a feast day, with a meal starting after church with *mezthes* (appetizers) and ending with sweet honey desserts, all showcasing Greece's hallmark ingredients: plump olives, feta cheese, flaky phyllo, yogurt, nuts, honey, and ouzo—a licorice-flavored liqueur used for toasting special occasions.

Mexican Christmas Buffet

Christmas is a colorful fiesta in Mexico, beginning with *posada* processions and ending with lively *piñata* parties.

Three-Pepper Quesadillas (recipe, page 55)

Black Bean Soup (recipe, page 30)

Christmas Eve Salad (recipe, page 31)

Chicken Mole

Guacamole (recipe, page 30)

Tomatillo Salsa

Steamed rice

Warm tortillas

Raisin Bread Pudding (recipe, page 110)

Frozen Margaritas (recipe, page 31)

Chicken Mole

Pollo en Mole Poblano

(POH-yoh en MOH-lay poh-BLAH-noh)

Prep: 1 hour Bake: 45 minutes

- 6 dried poblano, ancho, pasilla, or mulato chile peppers
- 1 6-inch corn tortilla
- ⅓ cup slivered almonds
- 2 tablespoons sesame seeds
- ¼ teaspoon anise seeds
- 1 7½-ounce can stewed tomatoes
- 1 medium onion, chopped (½ cup)
- ¼ cup raisins
- 1 ounce unsweetened chocolate, chopped
- 1 tablespoon sugar
- 1 clove garlic, minced
- 1¼ teaspoons salt
- ½ teaspoon ground cinnamon
- ½ teaspoon ground coriander
- ⅛ teaspoon ground black pepper
- ⅛ teaspoon ground cloves
- 2 tablespoons cooking oil
- 1¼ cups chicken broth
- 6 to 10 pounds meaty chicken or turkey pieces (breast halves, wings, thighs, and drumsticks)

1. Cover dried peppers with boiling water. soak for 30 minutes. Drain peppers. Remove seeds; chop peppers.*

2. Meanwhile, in a small skillet, toast tortilla over medium heat for 2 to 4 minutes or until light brown, turning once. Remove; tear into pieces. Add almonds to skillet; toast for 2 to 4 minutes or until light brown. Remove almonds. Add sesame seeds to skillet; toast for 1 to 3 minutes or until light brown. Remove sesame seeds. Add anise seeds to skillet; toast for 1 to 3 minutes or just until light brown. Remove anise seeds; crush and set aside.

3. For mole, in a food processor bowl, combine chopped peppers, tortilla pieces, almonds, sesame seeds, anise seeds, *undrained* tomatoes, onion, raisins, chocolate, sugar, garlic, salt, cinnamon, coriander, black pepper, and cloves. Cover and process until coarsely pureed. (Or add *half* of the mixture to a blender. Cover and blend until coarsely pureed. Transfer pureed mixture to a medium bowl. Repeat with remaining mixture.)

4. In a medium saucepan, heat *1 tablespoon* of the oil over medium heat. Add pureed mixture; cook and stir about 5 minutes or until darkened and thick. Slowly stir in chicken broth.

5. Preheat oven to 375°F for chicken or 325°F for turkey. In a 12-inch skillet, heat remaining oil over medium-high heat. Add *half* of the chicken; cook for 6 to 8 minutes or until brown, turning once. Place in a roasting pan. Repeat with remaining chicken. Coat chicken with *2 cups* of the mole.

6. Bake, covered, until meat is tender and juices are no longer pink (170°F for breast halves; 180°F for thighs and drumsticks), allowing 45 to 50 minutes for chicken or 1½ to 2¼ hours for turkey. Reheat remaining mole; serve with chicken. If desired, garnish with lime wedges and cilantro. Makes 8 to 12 servings.

*Note: Because chile peppers contain volatile oils that can burn your skin and eyes, avoid direct contact with them as much as possible. When working with chile peppers, wear plastic or rubber gloves. If your bare hands do touch the peppers, wash your hands and nails well with soap and warm water.

Tomatillo Salsa

Prep: 30 minutes Chill: 2 hours

- 8 ounces tomatoes, seeded and chopped
- 4 ounces fresh tomatillos, husked, rinsed, peeled, and chopped, or one 13-ounce can tomatillos, rinsed, drained, and chopped (about 1¼ cups)
- 1 small red onion, chopped (⅓ cup)
- 2 tablespoons snipped fresh cilantro
- 2 tablespoons lime juice
- 2 to 4 fresh serrano, habanero, jalapeño, or other hot chile peppers, seeded and finely chopped (see note, opposite)
- 4 cloves garlic, minced
- ¼ teaspoon salt

1. In a medium bowl, combine tomatoes, tomatillos, onion, cilantro, lime juice, chile peppers, garlic, and salt. Cover and chill for 2 hours to 1 week. Makes 2½ cups.

Mexican Christmas Buffet
(recipes, pages 28 to 31)

Guacamole
Pictured on page 29.
Start to finish: 15 minutes

    2   very ripe medium avocados, halved,
        seeded, peeled, and cut up
    ½   of a small onion, cut up
    ½   of a 4-ounce can (¼ cup) diced green
        chile peppers, drained, 2 fresh jalapeño
        chile peppers, seeded and chopped (see
        note, page 28), or several drops
        bottled hot pepper sauce
    1   tablespoon snipped fresh cilantro or
        parsley
    1   tablespoon lemon juice or lime juice
    1   clove garlic, minced
    ¼   teaspoon salt
    ⅔   cup finely chopped, peeled and seeded
        tomato (optional)
        Avocado slices (optional)

1. In a food processor bowl or blender container, combine avocados, onion, chile peppers, cilantro, lemon juice, garlic, and salt. Cover; process or blend until smooth, scraping side as necessary. If desired, stir in tomato and garnish with avocado slices. Makes 1 cup.

Make-Ahead Tip: Prepare Guacamole as directed, except do not stir in the tomato. Cover and chill for up to 24 hours. If desired, stir in tomato and garnish with avocado slices just before serving.

The *posada* and *piñata* are central to Mexico's Christmas celebration. Starting on December 16, families participate in posadas. While the word actually means "lodging," the *posada* is a candlelit procession from house to house, imitating the journey of Joseph and Mary. Those making the procession are turned away twice before being invited into the host's home, where they join a lively fiesta. Poinsettias and luminarias create a festive air and buffet tables groan with beloved Mexican dishes. After the big feast, it's time to break the *piñata*, a gaily decorated hollow figure. Children are blindfolded and given a stick to knock down the *piñata*. After several turns, the *piñata's* cache of candy spills out at the children's feet.

Black Bean Soup
Stand: 30 minutes Prep: 25 minutes
Cook: 30 minutes

    2   dried poblano, ancho, or chipotle chile
        peppers (see note, page 28)
    2   large green sweet peppers, chopped
        (2 cups)
    2   large onions, chopped (2 cups)
    4   cloves garlic, minced
    2   tablespoons olive oil or cooking oil
    4   15-ounce cans black beans, rinsed and
        drained
    2   14-ounce cans beef broth
    4   medium tomatoes, chopped (2 cups)
    ¼   cup snipped fresh cilantro or parsley
    2   tablespoons snipped fresh thyme or
        2 teaspoons dried thyme, crushed
    4   teaspoons snipped fresh oregano or
        1 teaspoon dried oregano, crushed
        Dairy sour cream (optional)
        Fresh cilantro sprigs (optional)

1. Cover dried peppers with boiling water; soak for 30 minutes. Drain peppers. Remove seeds; chop peppers.

2. In a 4-quart Dutch oven, cook sweet pepper, onion, and garlic in hot oil for 3 minutes. Stir in drained pepper pieces, black beans, beef broth, tomato, snipped cilantro, thyme, and oregano. Bring to boiling; reduce heat. Cover and simmer for 30 minutes.

3. If desired, mash beans slightly. If desired, garnish each serving with a spoonful of sour cream and cilantro sprigs. Makes 12 first-course or 6 main-dish servings.

Slow Cooker Directions: Prepare dried peppers as directed. Omit oil. In a 5- to 6-quart electric slow cooker, combine dried pepper pieces, sweet pepper, onion, garlic, black beans, beef broth, tomato, snipped cilantro, thyme, and oregano. Cover and cook on low-heat setting for 8 to 10 hours or on high-heat setting for 4 to 5 hours. Serve as directed.

*****Note:** For a pureed bean soup, cool soup slightly. Place *half* of the soup in a food processor bowl or blender container. Cover and process or blend until smooth. Repeat with remaining soup.

Christmas Eve Salad

Christmas Eve Salad
Ensalada de Noche Buena
(EN-sah-lah-dah day NOH-chay BWAY-nah)
Prep: 30 minutes Chill: 2 hours

⅓ cup olive oil
½ teaspoon finely shredded orange peel
¼ cup orange juice
2 tablespoons sugar
2 tablespoons dry sherry or lemon juice
Romaine leaves
3 medium oranges, peeled and sectioned
2 large apples, cored and sliced
2 medium bananas, sliced
1 16-ounce can sliced beets, rinsed and
    drained
½ cup pine nuts, toasted, or peanuts

1. For dressing, in a screw-top jar, combine olive oil, orange peel, orange juice, sugar, and sherry or lemon juice. Cover and shake well. Chill for 2 to 24 hours.

2. To serve, line a platter with romaine leaves; top with fruit, beets, and nuts. Shake dressing; pour over salad. Makes 8 first-course servings.

Frozen Margaritas
Pictured on page 29.
Stand: 30 minutes Prep: 20 minutes

4 large limes
½ cup sugar
1 cup tequila
¼ to ⅓ cup orange liqueur
1 cup ice cubes
Lime wedges (optional)
Coarse salt (optional)
Crushed ice

1. Finely shred lime peel. Stir peel into 2 cups *water*. Let stand for 30 to 60 minutes.

2. Strain lime peel through a sieve into a bowl; discard peel. Add sugar to liquid; stir until dissolved. Squeeze limes to make ½ cup juice; stir into liquid. Stir in tequila and orange liqueur.

3. Pour *half* of the mixture into a blender container; add *half* of the ice cubes. Cover; blend until chopped. Repeat. If desired, rub rims of glasses with lime wedges; dip into coarse salt. Pour tequila mixture over crushed ice. Makes 6 to 8 servings.

Our Heritage Table

THE OLD COUNTRY still influences our tastes at home, especially at Christmastime. Whether we stay true to our own roots or adopt a homeland through marriage, cherished pieces have their place on our family table and in our hearts. Yet within our melding traditions, there's much room to play, allowing us to blend a foreign accent with something contemporary, new, and fun. Our table accents show you how anything old-world can be new again. Elegant trimmings from afar offer easy and affordable ways to make your holiday gatherings memorable. Mix a few of our ideas with customs of your own, and your beautiful table will become an integral part of your family's holiday traditions.

Fresh fruit has been a gift of choice since the 1600s. Because it was a such a rarity during the holiday season, sharing it was considered a generous act. Offer your guests a contemporary version of this charming tradition by composing a simple fruit tree on your buffet. Stack two glass pedestal-style cake stands and a pedestal-style candy dish to create the shape of a Christmas tree. Fill each tier with plump and colorful winter fruits, then wrap with a garland of sparkling red edible berries.

Traditional elements can team with innovative ideas to make a classic table setting charming yet easy. Here, newer linens, china, and crystal blend with heirloom silverware. Together, they provide a neutral background for old-world touches. Also, French country chairs and a touch of toile fabric hint at a French connection that melds beautifully with the room's Russian red accents and ornate British Victorian flourishes.

Beaded Beauties. Place cards originally were introduced to the tabletop to facilitate seating parties of eight or more guests. Above, each place card is tucked inside a miniature picture frame (decorated with European-style beads) that can easily double as a party favor. For additional color at each place setting, string glass beads on curved wire to make a napkin ring (right). A crimp in each end of the wire holds the beads in place.

Wine Charms. A recent addition to American tabletops, wine charms offer a quick way to discern your glass from other guests' as you move around the room. Each charm below is made from a 1¼-inch wire earring hoop, available at most arts and crafts stores. A combination of silver buttons and glass beads decorates the hoop, which easily fits around a wine glass stem.

In these days of blending families and traditions, it's OK to set your table with a mix of treasured heirlooms and recent purchases. This table setting above combines new, modestly priced, silver-rimmed salad plates with circa-1920s dinner plates and sterling silver flatware that has been serving guests for generations. Mismatched sets of stemware, acquired over the decades, serve as water and wine goblets.

And in the center of it all? Flowers, of course. Until the mid-19th century, fresh flowers during the winter months were scarce and expensive. Seasonal greenery served as the botanical embellishment of choice. But, beginning in the 1830s, greenhouses in Europe and in the eastern United States began forcing blooms. Today, you can count on fresh flowers to make your holiday table come alive.

This easy-to-assemble centerpiece pairs two varieties of flowers: red amaryllis, a thick-stemmed flower grown in greenhouses at Christmastime, and white dendrobium orchids, flower-covered tendrils that are a florist's favorite in every season. Sprigs of evergreen and berries pay homage to more traditional floral arrangements.

The Christmas wreath, like the Christmas tree, symbolizes the strength of life overcoming the forces of winter. In ancient Rome, people hung wreaths as a sign of victory and celebration. The custom of hanging a Christmas wreath on the front door probably came from this practice. Here, windows are adorned with red berry wreaths. Paper-covered floral wires attach the wreaths to window fixtures for easy hanging.

Neutral Necessities. European tone-on-tone linens provide a complementary backdrop for any holiday table. Choose linens of varying textures, such as the large-patterned floral and the dotted Swiss print above—one to cover the entire table, the second to drape diagonally. For the bottom linen, measure your table surface and add approximately 18 inches to each dimension. For the top linen, add approximately 12 inches to the width and subtract approximately 15 inches from the length. Then stitch a tassel, purchased at a fabric shop, to each corner for an old-world look.

Cushy Color. Even your chairs can match the color scheme. To make complementary holiday seat covers, cut an inexpensive tablecloth into 24-inch squares. Unscrew the seats, wrap the fabric around each seat, and use painter's tape or staples to attach the fabric to the underside. Then pop the seat back into place.

During America's Victorian era, people sent messages of friendship, love, and good health with tussie-mussies. Convey the same warm wishes by tying one of these small, handheld arrangements to the back of each guest's chair (above). Our simple arrangement includes a single stem of deep red amaryllis and a few sprigs of white euphorbia, both commonly used in Christmas bouquets. To keep the flowers fresh, place the stems inside a simple plastic water tube covered by a sterling silver cone (or a paper doily stapled into the shape of a cone). Attach the cones to the chair backs with thin paper-wrapped floral wires and ribbons.

The Tasting Table

LITTLE NIBBLES enjoyed before a meal are a beloved tradition the world over. To the Greeks, they're *mezes*, and they're always meant to be shared. In Russia, little bites are appropriately named *zakuski*, meaning "to bite." The Spanish refer to their pre-dinner snacks as *tapas*. The French call them *hors d'oeuvres*. In China, they're *dim sum*, loosely translated as "heart's delight." And, Swedes delight in their *smorgasbord* of goodies. Americans call them *appetizers*, for they stimulate the appetite—and a good time. Join our world tour of festive little delicacies. After all, the best things come in small packages!

Baked Brie with Chutney Glaze
(recipe, page 43)

Brandied Pork Pâté

Prep: 30 minutes Bake: 1½ hours
Cool: 1 hour Chill: 8 hours

- 6 slices bacon
- 8 ounces chicken livers, drained
- 1 large onion, cut up
- 2 eggs
- ½ cup brandy
- 4 cloves garlic
- ¼ cup all-purpose flour
- 2 teaspoons paprika
- 2 teaspoons snipped fresh rosemary or 1 teaspoon dried rosemary, crushed
- ½ teaspoon salt
- ¼ teaspoon ground allspice
- ¼ teaspoon ground black pepper
- 1 pound ground pork
- 4 ounces ground cooked ham
- 2 bay leaves
- Fresh rosemary sprigs (optional)
- Toasted baguette slices or crackers

1. In a large skillet, cook bacon over medium heat until brown but still limp. Remove bacon, reserving *2 tablespoons* of the drippings in skillet. Drain bacon on paper towels; set aside.

2. In same skillet, cook livers in reserved drippings about 5 minutes or until no longer pink.

3. In a blender container or food processor bowl, combine chicken livers, onion, eggs, brandy, garlic, flour, paprika, snipped rosemary, salt, allspice, and pepper. Cover; blend or process until smooth. If using food processor, add pork and ham, scraping the side of the container as necessary; cover and process until mixed. (If using a blender, transfer liver mixture to a large bowl; add pork and ham and mix well.)

4. Preheat oven to 350°F. Lay bacon slices crosswise to cover bottom and sides of an 8×4×2-inch loaf pan. Spoon meat mixture into pan; press firmly. Top with bay leaves. Cover tightly with foil. Place on a baking sheet. Bake for 1½ hours.

5. Remove foil; drain well, keeping pâté in pan. Place pan on a wire rack; cover with heavy foil. Place weights (cans or dry beans) on foil. Cool for 1 hour at room temperature; chill with weights for 8 to 24 hours.

6. Remove the weights, foil, and bay leaves. Unmold pâté. If desired, garnish with rosemary. Serve with baguette slices. Makes 32 servings.

Onion-Olive Tart
Pissaladière (pee-sah-lah-DAIR)
Prep: 20 minutes Cook: 30 minutes
Bake: 12 minutes

- ¼ cup olive oil
- 5 cups sliced onions
- ½ teaspoon dried thyme, crushed
- ¼ teaspoon ground black pepper
- 2 large cloves garlic, minced
- 2 2-ounce cans anchovy fillets, drained
- 1 16-ounce loaf frozen white or wheat bread dough, thawed
- 2 ounces finely shredded Parmesan cheese (½ cup)
- ½ cup pitted ripe olives, halved

1. In a large skillet, heat *2 tablespoons* of the oil over medium-low heat. Add onion, thyme, and pepper; cook about 30 minutes or until onion is very tender and golden brown, stirring occasionally. Remove from heat; set aside.

2. In a small bowl, combine garlic and remaining *2 tablespoons* oil. Mash *six* of the anchovies; stir into oil mixture. Cut remaining anchovies into thin strips; set aside.

3. Preheat oven to 450°F. On a lightly floured surface, roll dough into a 12-inch square. (If too elastic, let rest a few minutes.) Grease a very large baking sheet; place dough on sheet, reshaping as needed. Brush with garlic mixture; sprinkle with *¼ cup* Parmesan, onions, remaining *¼ cup* Parmesan, anchovies, and olives.

4. Bake for 12 to 15 minutes or until crust is golden. Serve warm or cool. To serve, cut into squares. Makes 36 appetizers.

Quiche Lorraine Squares
Prep: 20 minutes Bake: 48 minutes
Cool: 15 minutes

- 1 recipe Quiche Pastry Dough (below)
- 2 slices bacon
- 1 large onion, chopped (1 cup)
- 8 eggs
- 2 cups half-and-half or light cream
- ¼ teaspoon ground black pepper
- Dash ground nutmeg
- 8 ounces Gruyère or Swiss cheese, shredded (2 cups)

1. Preheat oven to 425°F. On a lightly floured surface, using a floured rolling pin, roll Quiche Pastry Dough into a 17×12-inch rectangle. Fold into quarters; transfer to an ungreased 15×10×1-inch baking pan. Gently unfold dough, allowing extra pastry to overhang edges. (If pastry tears, press together with fingers.) Fold under extra pastry; press onto side of pan. Line with foil.

2. Bake for 15 minutes. Remove foil; bake about 8 minutes more or until pastry is golden. Cool on a wire rack.

3. In a medium skillet, cook bacon over medium heat until crisp. Remove bacon, reserving drippings in skillet; drain bacon on paper towels. Cook onion in reserved drippings until tender, stirring occasionally; set aside.

4. In a large bowl, whisk together eggs, half-and-half, pepper, and nutmeg until combined. Crumble bacon; sprinkle bacon, onion, and cheese evenly onto crust. Slowly pour egg mixture over bacon mixture.

5. Bake in a 350°F oven about 25 minutes or until filling is set and puffed around the edges. Cool in pan on a wire rack for 15 minutes. To serve, cut into squares. Makes 54 appetizers.

Quiche Pastry Dough: In a medium bowl, stir together 2 cups all-purpose flour and ½ teaspoon salt. Using a pastry blender, cut in ½ cup shortening and ¼ cup cold butter until pieces are pea-size. Sprinkle 1 tablespoon cold water over part of the mixture; gently toss with a fork. Push moistened dough to the side of the bowl. Repeat with an additional 5 to 6 tablespoons cold water, using 1 tablespoon water at a time, until all flour mixture is moistened. Form dough into a ball.

Grilled Cheese
Raclette (rah-KLEHT)
Prep: 15 minutes Stand: 1 hour
Chill: 4 hours Grill: 5 minutes

- 6 ounces process Gruyère or Swiss cheese, shredded or torn (1½ cups)
- 4 ounces Gouda cheese, shredded (1 cup)
- 1 tablespoon Dijon-style mustard
- Toasted baguette slices

1. In a medium bowl, combine cheeses; cover and let stand at room temperature for 1 hour.

2. Add mustard; beat with an electric mixer until combined (mixture will be crumbly). Form into a ball; shape into a 4½-inch round, about 1 inch thick. Wrap in plastic wrap; chill for 4 to 24 hours.

3. Unwrap cheese; cut into six wedges. Place in a 6-inch cast-iron skillet, separating slightly.

4. To grill, place skillet on grill rack directly over low coals; grill for 5 to 7 minutes or until softened and heated through. To bake, bake in a 400°F oven for 5 to 7 minutes or until soft. Serve warm with baguette slices. Makes 6 servings.

Baked Brie with Chutney Glaze
Pictured on page 40.
Prep: 10 minutes Bake: 20 minutes

- 1 wheel (2 to 2¼ pounds) Brie cheese
- ½ cup mango chutney
- Pear and/or apple slices

1. Preheat oven to 325°F. Place cheese on an oven-going platter or baking sheet. Spread chutney on top. Bake, uncovered, for 20 minutes.

2. Carefully transfer cheese to a platter. Serve immediately with fruit. Makes 16 to 20 servings.

Brie, perhaps the most known and loved of French cheeses, hails from the Ile de France region that surrounds Paris. American cooks have discovered the delights of serving Brie warmed (its oozy translucence is irresistible!) and slathered with a variety of preserves or spreads. The delicious variations on this easy theme are endless—including the chutney-topped version above.

Parmesan Pastry Spirals and
Cheddar Cheese Wafers

Parmesan Pastry Spirals
Parmesan Palmiers (pahlm-YAYZ)
Prep: 10 minutes Freeze: 30 minutes
Bake: 12 minutes

- ½ of a 17.3-ounce package (1 sheet) frozen puff pastry sheets, thawed
- 1 tablespoon milk
- 2 ounces finely shredded Parmesan cheese (½ cup)

1. On a lightly floured surface, roll pastry into a 14×10-inch rectangle. Brush with milk; sprinkle with ⅓ cup Parmesan. Starting at a short side, loosely roll into a spiral, stopping at center. Repeat from other side. (Rolls will meet in center.) Wrap in plastic wrap; freeze 30 minutes.

2. Preheat oven to 350°F. Line two baking sheets with parchment paper; set aside. Remove wrap from pastry; place roll on a cutting board. Cut crosswise into ⅜-inch-thick slices. Arrange slices on prepared baking sheets, reshaping as needed. Top with remaining milk and Parmesan.

3. Bake for 12 to 14 minutes or until golden. Transfer to a rack. Serve warm. Makes 24 spirals.

Make-Ahead Tip: Prepare Parmesan Pastry Spirals as directed, except freeze in wrap for up to 8 hours. Thaw for 30 minutes. Unwrap, slice, and bake as directed.

Cheddar Cheese Wafers
Prep: 30 minutes Chill: 3 hours
Bake: 10 minutes

- 1 cup butter, softened
- 8 ounces sharp cheddar cheese, shredded (2 cups)
- 2 teaspoons Worcestershire sauce
- 2 cups all-purpose flour
- ¼ teaspoon salt
- ¼ teaspoon cayenne pepper
- 2 egg yolks
- 2 tablespoons milk
- ¼ cup finely chopped walnuts (optional)

1. In a large bowl, beat butter and cheese with an electric mixer on medium speed until light and fluffy. Beat in Worcestershire sauce just until combined. Add flour, salt, and cayenne pepper, beating on low speed until mixed.

2. Form dough into a ball. Divide in half; shape each half into a 2-inch-wide log. Wrap each in plastic wrap. Chill for 3 to 24 hours.

3. Preheat oven to 375°F. In a small bowl, whisk together egg yolks and milk. Cut logs into ¼-inch-thick slices. Arrange slices on ungreased baking sheets; brush tops with egg yolk mixture. If desired, sprinkle with nuts.

4. Bake for 10 to 12 minutes or until golden. Cool on wire rack. Makes 48 wafers.

Make-Ahead Tip: Prepare and bake Cheddar Cheese Wafers as directed. Place wafers in freezer container; freeze for up to 1 month. To serve, thaw at room temperature.

Sausage Pastry Rolls
Prep: 30 minutes Bake: 20 minutes

- 1 17.3-ounce package (2 sheets) frozen puff pastry sheets, thawed
- 1 pound bulk pork sausage
- ¼ cup snipped fresh parsley or chopped green onion
- 1 egg

1. On a lightly floured surface, roll out each sheet of pastry to a 12-inch square.

2. In a bowl, combine sausage and parsley. Divide in half; shape into two 12-inch-long logs.

3. Preheat oven to 375°F. Place a sausage log near edge of each pastry square. Roll pastry around sausage to enclose log. Beat egg; brush onto seam; press to seal.

4. Using a serrated knife, cut each sausage roll into 2-inch-wide slices. Place slices, seam sides down, on an ungreased 15×10×1-inch baking pan. Brush with remaining egg.

5. Bake for 20 to 25 minutes or until sausage is done (an instant-read thermometer inserted into center registers 160°F). Makes 12 rolls.

Sausage Pastry Rolls were inspired by the Cornish pasty (pronounced PASS-tee), a turnover made of meat and potatoes baked in a pastry. This "meal in a crust" provided lunchtime fare for miners working in the Cornwall area of England in the 18th and 19th centuries. Our easy bite-size version is perfect for a holiday tea or appetizer party. Serve with a hot English mustard.

Swiss Cheese Fondue
Start to finish: 50 minutes

- 12 ounces Gruyère or Swiss cheese, shredded (3 cups)
- 8 ounces Emmentaler, Gruyère, or Swiss cheese, shredded (2 cups)
- 12 1-inch-thick slices French bread, cut into 1-inch cubes, and/or broccoli or cauliflower florets
- 1½ cups dry white wine
- 3 tablespoons all-purpose flour
- ¼ cup milk
- 2 tablespoons kirsch or dry sherry
- ⅛ teaspoon ground white pepper
- ⅛ teaspoon ground nutmeg
- Toasted bread cubes and/or vegetables

1. In a medium bowl, combine cheeses; cover and let stand at room temperature for 30 minutes.

2. Meanwhile, place bread cubes on a baking sheet. Bake in a 350°F oven for 5 to 7 minutes or until crisp and light brown; set aside.

3. In a medium saucepan, bring a small amount of water to boiling; add florets. Cover and simmer about 3 minutes or until crisp-tender. Drain; rinse with cold water. Set aside.

4. In a large saucepan, heat wine over medium heat until small bubbles rise to the surface. Just before wine boils, reduce heat to low.

5. Toss cheeses with flour. Stir cheese mixture into wine, a little at a time, stirring constantly and making sure cheese is melted before adding more. Stir until mixture bubbles gently. Stir in milk, kirsch or sherry, white pepper, and nutmeg.

6. Transfer cheese mixture to a fondue pot. Keep mixture bubbling gently over a fondue burner. (If mixture becomes too thick, stir in a little more milk.) Serve with toasted bread cubes and/or vegetables. Makes 3½ cups fondue (12 appetizer servings).

Creamy Meatballs
Start to finish: 30 minutes

- 1 pound ground beef
- 1 12-ounce can (1½ cups) evaporated milk
- ¼ cup fine dry bread crumbs
- ¼ cup finely chopped onion
- ½ teaspoon ground allspice
- ¼ teaspoon salt
- Dash ground black pepper
- 3 tablespoons butter or margarine
- 1 teaspoon instant beef bouillon granules
- 1 cup boiling water
- 2 tablespoons all-purpose flour
- 1 tablespoon Worcestershire sauce

1. In a large bowl, combine ground beef, ⅔ *cup* of the evaporated milk, the bread crumbs, onion, allspice, salt, and pepper. Shape meat mixture into 40 meatballs.

2. In a 12-inch skillet, melt butter over medium heat. Add meatballs. Cook, turning frequently, until done (an instant-read thermometer inserted into a meatball registers 160°F). Remove meatballs, reserving 1 *tablespoon* of the drippings in skillet; drain meatballs on paper towels.

3. Dissolve bouillon in boiling water. Stir flour into drippings in skillet; stir in bouillon, remaining evaporated milk, and Worcestershire sauce. Cook and stir over medium heat until thickened and bubbly. Cook and stir for 1 minute more. Return meatballs to skillet; heat through. Makes 20 servings.

Smoked Salmon in Dill Cream
Prep: 15 minutes Chill: 4 hours

- 1 8-ounce package cream cheese, softened
- ¼ cup half-and-half, light cream, or milk
- 3 green onions, chopped
- 1 tablespoon lemon juice
- 4 to 6 dashes bottled hot pepper sauce
- 2 tablespoons snipped fresh dill or 1 teaspoon dried dill weed
- 6 ounces smoked salmon, flaked
- Fresh dill sprigs (optional)
- Crackers or rye bread

1. In a medium bowl, combine softened cream cheese and half-and-half; stir with a fork until smooth. Add green onions, lemon juice, hot pepper sauce, and snipped dill; stir until combined. Fold in smoked salmon. Cover and chill for 4 to 24 hours.

2. If desired, garnish with dill sprigs. Serve with crackers or rye bread. Makes 16 servings.

Smoked Salmon in Dill Cream

Smoked salmon is a specialty of many northern countries surrounded by salmon-filled waters, including Norway, Ireland, Scotland, and Canada. With dill in the creamy mix, this sumptuous spread is inspired by traditions in Scandinavia, where smoked salmon is enjoyed year-round, but often is a much-loved part of the Christmas buffet table. If you use the drier hot-smoked salmon in the recipe opposite, flake it with a fork. If you use the moist lox-style smoked salmon, slice it into thin strips.

Bacon-Onion Crescents are inspired by the little savory pies known as *piradzini* in Russia, where cooks sometimes serve them as a clever way to use leftover vegetables and meats. Baked or fried, these little bites sometimes appear on an appetizer table, along with other delicacies such as Cheese Tarts. These are almost always accompanied by what the Russians call "little water"—known in our country as vodka.

Cheese Tarts
Vatrushki (vah-TRUSH-kee)
Prep: 45 minutes Chill: 2 hours
Bake: 20 minutes Cool: 5 minutes

- 1 8-ounce package cream cheese, softened
- 1 cup dry-curd cottage cheese
- 1 8-ounce carton dairy sour cream
- 2 eggs
- 1 recipe Sour Cream Pastry (right)

Dairy sour cream (optional)
Red and/or black caviar (optional)

1. For filling, in a medium bowl, combine cream cheese, cottage cheese, ⅓ *cup* of the sour cream, and *one* of the eggs. Beat with an electric mixer on medium speed until combined. Cover; chill for 2 hours.

2. Preheat oven to 375°F. To assemble tarts, on a lightly floured surface, roll Sour Cream Pastry to slightly less than ⅛-inch thickness. Using a 2½-inch fluted round cutter, cut out dough. Gently press rounds into 1¾-inch muffin pans. Spoon about *1 tablespoon* of the filling into each.

3. Bake about 20 minutes or until pastry is golden and filling is puffed. Cool for 5 minutes in pans; remove from pans. Serve warm. If desired, garnish with additional sour cream and caviar. Makes about 30 tarts.

Sour Cream Pastry: In a medium bowl, stir together 2 cups all-purpose flour and ¼ teaspoon salt. Using a pastry blender, cut in 6 tablespoons butter until pieces are pea-size. Make a well in the center. Add remaining sour cream. Slightly beat remaining egg; stir into flour mixture until combined. Form dough into a ball. Cover with plastic wrap; chill about 30 minutes or until dough is easy to handle.

Bacon-Onion Crescents
Piradzini (peh-RAWD-zee-nee)
Prep: 1 hour Rise: 1½ hours
Bake: 12 minutes

- 3¼ to 3½ cups all-purpose flour
- 1 package active dry yeast
- 1 cup milk
- 2 tablespoons sugar
- 2 tablespoons shortening
- ½ teaspoon salt
- 2 eggs
- 12 ounces sliced bacon, finely chopped
- ¾ cup chopped onion
- ⅛ teaspoon ground black pepper

1. In a large bowl, stir together 1½ cups of the flour and the yeast; set aside.

2. In small saucepan, heat and stir milk, sugar, shortening, and salt until warm (120°F to 130°F) and shortening is almost melted. Stir into flour mixture; add *one* egg. Beat with an electric mixer on low speed for 30 seconds. Beat on high for 3 minutes, scraping bowl often. Using a wooden spoon, stir in as much remaining flour as you can.

3. Turn out onto a lightly floured surface. Knead in enough remaining flour to make a moderately stiff dough that is smooth and elastic (6 to 8 minutes total). Shape into a ball. Place in a lightly greased bowl; turn once. Cover; let rise in a warm place until double (about 1 hour).

4. Meanwhile, for filling, in a skillet, cook bacon until crisp; remove bacon, reserving *2 tablespoons* drippings in skillet. Drain on paper towels. Cook onion in reserved drippings until tender, stirring often; drain. Add onion to bacon; sprinkle with pepper. Cover; chill until needed.

5. Punch down dough; turn out onto a lightly floured surface. Divide into thirds. Cover; let rest for 10 minutes. Lightly grease two large baking sheets; set aside.

6. Divide each dough portion into 12 pieces. Shape each into a ball; roll into a 3-inch round. Arrange rounds on prepared sheets. Cover; let rise until nearly double (about 30 minutes).

7. Preheat oven to 375°F. Place *1 rounded teaspoon* of the filling in center of each round. Fold dough over filling to enclose. With the tines of a fork, seal edges. Prick tops. Beat remaning egg; brush onto tops. Bake for 12 to 15 minutes or until golden. Serve warm. Makes 36 crescents.

Crab Dumplings
Start to finish: 30 minutes

- 6 ounces fresh or frozen cooked crabmeat, thawed and drained (1 cup)
- ½ of an 8-ounce tub cream cheese with chives and onion, softened
- ⅓ cup chopped leek
- 1 tablespoon white wine Worcestershire sauce
- 24 pot sticker or wonton wrappers (about 6 ounces)

1. For filling, in a bowl, stir together crabmeat, cream cheese, leek, and Worcestershire sauce.

2. For each dumpling, place *1 rounded tablespoon* of the crab filling in center of each pot sticker or wonton wrapper. Brush edges with water; place a second wrapper over first, pressing edges to seal. If desired, trim edges with fluted pastry wheel.

3. In a 4-quart Dutch oven, cook dumplings, *six* at a time, in a large amount of gently boiling, lightly salted water for 2 to 2½ minutes or just until tender. (Don't let water boil vigorously.) Use a slotted spoon to remove dumplings.

4. Place cooked dumplings in a single layer on lightly greased baking sheet. Cover loosely with foil. Keep warm in a 300°F oven while cooking remaining dumplings. Makes 12 appetizers.

Make-Ahead Tip: Prepare and fill the Crab Dumplings as directed through step 2. Place filled dumplings on foil-lined baking sheets. Cover and freeze. Transfer frozen dumplings to freezer bags; seal, label, and freeze for up to 3 months. Cook frozen dumplings as directed in step 3 about 3 minutes or just until tender.

These Asian-inspired dumplings are wildly popular in our country, but they're not a traditional Chinese dish. Their true origins are up for grabs. Yet people can't seem to get enough of them. Boiled or fried, they're often second only to egg rolls as the most often-ordered appetizer in Chinese restaurants. So if you're looking for a surefire crowd-pleaser, you've found it!

Shrimp Sushi
Start to finish: 1¼ hours

- ½ cup short grain rice
- 1 cup cold water
- ¼ teaspoon salt
- 4 teaspoons rice vinegar or 1 tablespoon white vinegar
- 1½ teaspoons sugar
- 1 medium cucumber
- 1 pound (21 to 25 total) frozen peeled, cooked shrimp with tails, thawed
- ½ cup thinly sliced pickled ginger
- Green onion tops, cut into thin strips
- Wasabi paste (optional)

1. Wash rice under cold running water, rubbing grains together with fingers, until water runs clear; drain. In a small saucepan, combine rice, water, and salt. Bring just to boiling; reduce heat. Cover and simmer about 15 minutes or until liquid is absorbed. Remove from heat. Stir in vinegar and sugar. Cover; let stand until cool.

2. Using a lemon zester or fork, score cucumber lengthwise. Cut cucumber into ¼-inch-thick slices.

3. With moistened fingers, mold *1 scant tablespoon* of the rice mixture into a patty; repeat with remaining rice mixture.

4. Place a rice patty on top of each cucumber slice. Top each patty with a shrimp, a small piece of ginger, and green onion strips. If desired, serve with wasabi paste. Makes 21 to 25 appetizers.

Many people think that sushi refers to raw fish when, in fact, it refers to a seasoned rice mixture that's rolled or layered with seafood (cooked or raw), vegetables, and other ingredients. Here, the rice mixture is served, canapé style, on cucumber slices and topped with shrimp that's definitely cooked. A little green onion, some pickled ginger, and a dab of wasabi (a Japanese-style horseradish) complete this pretty holiday treat.

Tropical Spring Rolls
Start to finish: 1 hour

- ¼ cup lime juice
- 2 tablespoons soy sauce
- 1 tablespoon peanut oil or cooking oil
- 2 teaspoons grated fresh ginger
- 1 teaspoon sugar
- ½ teaspoon crushed red pepper
- 12 ounces cooked chicken, finely chopped (about 2½ cups)
- 1 cup warm water
- 12 8-inch round rice papers
- 60 fresh cilantro leaves
- ¾ cup jicama cut into thin strips
- 1 medium mango, peeled, seeded, and finely chopped
- 6 green onions, sliced
- Fresh cilantro sprigs (optional)
- Soy sauce or bottled sweet-and-sour sauce (optional)

1. In a medium bowl, combine lime juice, soy sauce, oil, ginger, sugar, and red pepper. Add chicken; toss gently to coat.

2. Pour 1 cup warm water into a pie plate. Carefully dip rice papers, *one* at a time, into warm water. Place papers, not touching, on clean dry kitchen towels. Let soften for a few minutes or until pliable.

3. Arrange *five* cilantro leaves in a row across lower third of *one* of the rice papers. Top with a generous *2 tablespoons* of the chicken and *1 tablespoon* each of the jicama, mango, and green onion. Fold in the ends. Beginning at the edge with the cilantro, tightly roll up the rice paper. Place, seam side down, on a cutting board. Cover with a damp towel. Repeat with the remaining rice paper and fillings.

4. To serve, diagonally cut each roll into thirds; arrange on a platter. If desired, garnish with additional cilantro; serve with desired dipping sauce. Makes 36 servings.

Make-Ahead Tip: Prepare Tropical Spring Rolls as directed. Cover and chill in the refrigerator for up to 4 hours. Serve as directed.

Cilantro Grilled Shrimp

The marinade in **Cilantro Grilled Shrimp** is based on a Moroccan specialty called *charmoula*. This sauce is little like an Italian pesto; both are traditionally made of herbs pressed into a paste and bound with olive oil and other ingredients. In the Moroccan classic, cilantro—rather than basil—is the starring herb. Here, *charmoula* is brushed onto grilled shrimp for a tantalizing holiday appetizer.

Cilantro Grilled Shrimp

Prep: 10 minutes Marinate: 20 minutes
Grill: 7 minutes

  2½ to 3 pounds (50 to 63 total) fresh or
      frozen large shrimp in shells
  ½ cup snipped fresh parsley
  ½ cup snipped fresh cilantro
  ½ cup olive oil or cooking oil
  ½ cup lemon juice
  6 cloves garlic
  1 tablespoon paprika
  2 teaspoons ground cumin
  ½ teaspoon salt
  ½ teaspoon cayenne pepper
  ¼ teaspoon ground black pepper
  Lemon slices (optional)

1. Thaw shrimp, if frozen. Peel and devein shrimp, leaving tails intact. Rinse shrimp; pat dry with paper towels. Set aside.

2. In a blender container, combine parsley, cilantro, oil, lemon juice, garlic, paprika, cumin, salt, cayenne pepper, and black pepper. Cover; blend until smooth, scraping side of container.

3. In a bowl, stir together shrimp and oil mixture. Cover; marinate in the refrigerator for 20 to 30 minutes.

4. Drain shrimp, reserving marinade. Thread shrimp onto skewers. To grill, arrange shrimp on rack of an uncovered grill directly over medium coals. Grill for 7 to 9 minutes or until shrimp turn pink, turning often and brushing with reserved marinade. If desired, garnish with lemon slices and additional cilantro. Makes 12 to 16 servings.

Stuffed Phyllo Triangles
Prep: 1 hour Bake: 12 minutes

½ of a 16-ounce package (twenty 9x14-inch sheets) frozen phyllo dough, thawed
½ cup butter, melted
1 recipe Feta Cheese Filling or Spinach-Cheese Filling (right)

1. Unroll phyllo dough; cover with plastic wrap to prevent drying. Place *one* of the phyllo sheets on a work surface; brush lightly with some of the melted butter. Place another phyllo sheet on top of the first; brush with butter. Cut the layered sheets crosswise into 6×3-inch strips.

2. Preheat oven to 375°F. For each triangle, spoon about *1 tablespoon* of the Feta Cheese Filling or Spinach-Cheese Filling about 1 inch from a short edge of a strip. Bring a corner of the short edge over filling so the short edge lines up with a long edge, forming a triangle. Continue folding to end of strip. Repeat with remaining sheets of phyllo, butter, and filling.

3. Place triangles on an ungreased baking sheet; brush with any remaining butter. Bake for 12 to 15 minutes or until golden. Cool slightly on a wire rack. Serve warm. Makes 36 triangles.

Feta Cheese Filling: In a medium bowl, beat 1 egg. Stir in 6 ounces crumbled feta cheese (1½ cups), ¾ cup cream-style cottage cheese, 3 tablespoons snipped fresh dill or parsley, 2 tablespoons finely shredded Parmesan cheese, 4 teaspoons cornstarch, and ¼ teaspoon ground black pepper.

Spinach-Cheese Filling: Wash 10 ounces fresh spinach leaves; chop. In a covered medium saucepan, steam spinach about 3 minutes or until wilted (do not add any additional water). (Or thaw one 10-ounce package frozen chopped spinach.) Drain spinach and squeeze dry with paper towels; set aside. In a medium skillet, cook and stir ¾ cup finely chopped onion and ¼ cup sliced green onion in 1 tablespoon olive oil over medium heat about 5 minutes or until tender. Add spinach; cook until moisture is evaporated, stirring occasionally. Transfer to a medium bowl. Stir in 3 ounces crumbled feta cheese (¾ cup), ¼ cup cream-style cottage cheese, 2 tablespoons snipped fresh dill or parsley, 2 tablespoons fine dry bread crumbs, 1 beaten egg, and ¼ teaspoon ground black pepper.

Make-Ahead Tip: Prepare Stuffed Phyllo Triangles as directed through step 2. Place triangles on an ungreased baking sheet; brush with remaining butter. Cover and freeze until firm. Transfer to a freezer container or freezer bag; seal, label, and freeze for up to 1 month. To serve, place frozen triangles on a baking sheet; bake as directed in step 3.

Herbed Rice-Stuffed Grape Leaves and Stuffed Phyllo Triangles

Filled grape leaves are also called *dolmas* or *dolmades*, derived from an Arabic word referring to something that is stuffed. The Greek specialty originated after the destruction of Thebes, in the fourth century B.C., when cooks were forced to find ways to stretch tiny bits of meats. In later years, the recipes became more refined with the addition of nuts, dried fruits, and spices.

Herbed Rice-Stuffed Grape Leaves

Dolmades (dohl-MAH-dayz)

Prep: 40 minutes Steam: 10 minutes
Chill: 2 hours

- 1 cup water
- ½ cup long grain rice
- ¼ teaspoon salt
- 1 medium onion, chopped (½ cup)
- ¼ cup thinly sliced green onion
- 1 tablespoon olive oil
- 2 tablespoons golden raisins, chopped
- 2 tablespoons pine nuts
- 2 tablespoons snipped fresh parsley (reserve stems)
- 2 tablespoons lemon juice
- 1 tablespoon snipped fresh mint (reserve stems)
- 1 tablespoon snipped fresh dill (reserve stems)
- Dash ground cinnamon
- ⅓ of a 16-ounce jar (20 to 24 leaves) grape leaves, drained
- 1 3-inch piece stick cinnamon
- 1 recipe Cucumber-Yogurt Sauce

1. In a medium saucepan, combine water, rice, and salt. Bring to boiling; reduce heat. Cover and simmer for 15 minutes. Remove from heat; let stand for 5 minutes.

2. In a large saucepan, cook chopped onion and green onion in hot oil until onion is tender, stirring occasionally. Remove from heat. Stir in cooked rice, raisins, pine nuts, parsley, lemon juice, mint, dill, and ground cinnamon.

3. Separate and rinse grape leaves. Cut off and reserve stems; cut large leaves in half. In a large skillet, combine any damaged grape leaves, reserved grape leaf and herb stems, and stick cinnamon. Place a steamer basket in skillet. Add water to just below bottom of steamer basket.

4. To fill grape leaves, place them on a work surface with the rough sides up. Spoon *1 rounded tablespoon* of the rice mixture onto the center of each leaf. Fold bottom edges of leaves over filling; fold in sides. Starting from the bottom, tightly roll each into a spiral. Place rolled leaves, point sides down, in the steamer basket, arranging them close together in layers.

5. Bring water in skillet to boiling. Cover steamer; reduce heat. Steam rolls for 10 minutes. Remove steamer basket of rolls from skillet. Drain; discard leaves, stems, and cinnamon. Cool rolls; transfer to a covered container. Chill for at least 2 hours.

6. To serve, let stand at room temperature for 30 minutes, if desired. Serve with Cucumber-Yogurt Sauce. Makes 20 to 24 servings.

Cucumber-Yogurt Sauce: In a small bowl, stir together one 8-ounce carton plain yogurt, ¼ cup shredded cucumber, 1 tablespoon snipped fresh dill, and ¼ teaspoon finely shredded lemon peel.

Make-Ahead Tip: Prepare Herbed Rice-Stuffed Grape Leaves and Cucumber-Yogurt Sauce as directed. Transfer to separate airtight containers; refrigerate rolls for up to 3 days and sauce for up to 8 hours.

Marinated Olives

Prep: 15 minutes Chill: 8 hours

- 1¾ cups pitted green olives
- 1¾ cups pitted kalamata olives or pitted ripe olives
- ¼ cup olive oil
- 1 teaspoon finely shredded lemon peel
- 1 tablespoon lemon juice
- 3 cloves garlic, thinly sliced
- 1 tablespoon snipped fresh oregano or 1 teaspoon dried oregano, crushed
- 1 tablespoon snipped fresh rosemary or 1 teaspoon dried rosemary, crushed
- 1 tablespoon snipped fresh thyme or 1 teaspoon dried thyme, crushed
- Dash crushed red pepper

1. In a medium bowl, combine olives, oil, lemon peel, lemon juice, garlic, oregano, rosemary, thyme, and crushed red pepper; toss to coat. Cover and chill for 8 to 24 hours.

2. To serve, drain olives, discarding marinade. Transfer to a serving dish. Makes 16 servings.

Olive-Chicken Turnovers
Empanaditas de Pollo
(em-pah-NAH-dee-tahz day POH-yoh)
Prep: 50 minutes Chill: 30 minutes
Bake: 15 minutes

- **1** medium onion, finely chopped (½ cup)
- **2** cloves garlic, minced
- **1** tablespoon olive oil
- **1** cup bottled chunky salsa
- **5** ounces cooked chicken, finely chopped (1 cup)
- **⅓** cup finely chopped green sweet pepper
- **¼** cup chopped pimiento-stuffed olives
- **¼** teaspoon ground black pepper
- **1** recipe Turnover Pastry (below)
- **1** egg, slightly beaten

1. For filling, in a large skillet, cook onion and garlic in hot oil until tender. Stir in salsa, chicken, sweet pepper, olives, and black pepper. Cook, uncovered, about 2 minutes or until liquid has evaporated. Cool. Spread onto a baking sheet. Cover and chill for 30 minutes.

2. On a lightly floured surface, roll each ball of Turnover Pastry to ⅛-inch thickness. Using a 3-inch cutter, cut into 3-inch rounds.

3. Place *1 rounded teaspoon* of filling onto half of each circle. Brush edges with water. Fold other half of each circle over filling. Seal with tines of a fork. Reroll pastry as necessary. Keep pastry covered to prevent from drying.

4. Arrange turnovers on ungreased baking sheet. Prick tops with a fork. Brush with egg. Bake in a 375°F oven for 15 to 20 minutes or until golden. Serve warm. Makes 36 turnovers.

Turnover Pastry: In a large bowl, stir together 3 cups all-purpose flour and ¾ teaspoon salt. Cut in 1 cup lard or shortening until pieces are pea-size. Sprinkle 1 tablespoon cold water over part of the mixture; gently toss with a fork. Push to side of bowl. Repeat with 8 to 11 more tablespoons cold water, 1 tablespoon at a time, until all is moistened. Form into two balls.

Make-Ahead Tip: Prepare Olive-Chicken Turnovers as directed; cool 30 minutes. Place in a single layer on an ungreased baking sheet; freeze. Seal, label, and freeze in a freezer container up to 3 months. To reheat, arrange frozen turnovers on an ungreased baking sheet. Bake in a 375°F oven for 8 to 10 minutes or until heated through.

Avocado Chicken Tarts
Chilapitas de Pollo
(chee-lah-PEE-tahz day POH-yoh)
Prep: 25 minutes Bake: 14 minutes

- **1** recipe Cheese Pastry Dough (below)
- **8** ounces chopped, cooked chicken (1½ cups)
- **½** cup dairy sour cream or light dairy sour cream
- **½** cup seeded, peeled, and diced avocado
- **2** tablespoons snipped fresh cilantro
- **4** teaspoons chopped green onion
- **2** to 3 teaspoons finely chopped canned chipotle peppers in adobo sauce (see note, opposite)
- **¾** teaspoon finely shredded lime peel or lemon peel
- **2** teaspoons lime juice or lemon juice
- **Salt**
- **Ground black pepper**

1. Preheat oven to 375°F. Shape Cheese Pastry Dough into 16 balls; press into 2½- to 3-inch tart pans. (Or shape into 24 balls and press into 2½-inch muffin cups.) Bake for 14 to 16 minutes or until golden.

2. In a large bowl, stir together chicken, sour cream, avocado, snipped cilantro, green onion, chipotle peppers, peel, and juice. Season to taste with salt and black pepper.

3. To serve, fill warm Cheese Pastry Shells with chicken filling. Makes 16 to 24 tarts.

Cheese Pastry Dough: In a medium bowl, combine ⅓ cup butter and 3 ounces crumbled queso fresco or goat cheese (chèvre); beat with an electric mixer on medium speed until smooth. Beat in ¾ cup all-purpose flour and ¾ cup tortilla flour or yellow cornmeal. Add enough cold water (2 to 3 tablespoons) to form a soft dough. Shape into a ball.

Make-Ahead Tip: Bake pastry shells as directed; do not fill. Place pastry shells in an airtight container. Store in the refrigerator for up to 3 days or in the freezer for up to 1 month. To serve, thaw frozen shells at room temperature. Arrange chilled or thawed pastry shells on a baking sheet; heat in a 300°F oven for 5 minutes. Prepare filling as directed; fill pastry shells.

Shrimp and Tomato Pizzettas
Prep: 20 minutes Bake: 9 minutes

1   10-ounce package refrigerated pizza dough
3   medium plum tomatoes, sliced
1   6-ounce package frozen peeled, cooked shrimp (halve larger shrimp lengthwise)
2   tablespoons snipped fresh oregano
⅛   teaspoon crushed red pepper
3   ounces shredded four-cheese Italian-blend cheese or mozzarella cheese, (¾ cup)
Fresh oregano sprigs (optional)

1. Lightly grease a baking sheet; set aside. On a lightly floured surface, unroll pizza dough. Roll into a 13½×9-inch rectangle. Cut dough into six 4½-inch squares. Arrange squares about 1 inch apart on prepared baking sheet. If desired, fold over about ¼ inch of the dough on each edge; press with a fork. Bake in a 425°F oven for 4 to 5 minutes or until golden.

2. Divide tomato slices and shrimp among squares. Sprinkle with snipped oregano and red pepper. Sprinkle with cheese. Bake for 5 to 6 minutes more or until cheese is melted. If desired, garnish with fresh oregano sprigs. Makes 6 servings.

Shrimp and Tomato Pizzettas

Did you know that pizza has origins in Egypt? The cheese-topped classic then became popular in Italy, where American soldiers tasted it and brought the concept home with them after World War II. Now pizza is an all-American favorite and travels the world in a variety of versions. Here it's dressed up for the holidays with creative, fresh ingredients that would make any Italian cook proud.

Three-Pepper Quesadillas
Start to finish: 20 minutes

4   7- to 8-inch flour tortillas
Cooking oil or nonstick cooking spray
3   ounces Monterey Jack, queso quesadilla, Chihuahua, and/or asadero cheese, shredded (¾ cup)
½   cup canned black beans, rinsed and drained
¼   cup roasted red sweet peppers (see note, page 57), cut into thin strips
2   medium pepperoncini salad peppers, drained, seeded, and cut into strips
½   to 1 fresh jalapeño pepper,* seeded and thinly sliced, or 1 tablespoon canned sliced jalapeño peppers, drained
Dairy sour cream (optional)

1. Lightly brush *one* side of each tortilla with cooking oil or coat with nonstick cooking spray.

2. Place *two* tortillas, uncoated side up. Top with cheese, beans, roasted pepper strips, pepperoncini pepper strips, and jalapeño slices. Top with remaining tortillas, oiled sides up.

3. Heat a heavy skillet or griddle over medium heat. Cook quesadillas, one at a time, for 2 to 4 minutes or until cheese is melted and tortillas are golden, turning once.

4. Cut each quesadilla into eight wedges; serve warm. If desired, serve with sour cream. Makes 8 servings.

*Note: Because chile peppers contain volatile oils that can burn your skin and eyes, avoid direct contact with them as much as possible. When working with chile peppers, wear plastic or rubber gloves. If your bare hands do touch peppers, wash your hands well with soap and warm water.

Crostini is simply the Italian word for "little toast," but the word has also come to mean canapé-style appetizers made from toasts topped in a variety of ways. In this robust recipe, using white balsamic vinegar instead of regular balsamic vinegar lets the color appeal of the red and yellow sweet peppers come through better.

White Bean Spread
Start to finish: 15 minutes

1 medium onion, chopped (½ cup)
1 clove garlic, minced
½ teaspoon dried oregano, crushed
1½ teaspoons olive oil
1 15-ounce can great northern beans, rinsed and drained
1 tablespoon balsamic vinegar
⅛ teaspoon crushed red pepper
Armenian cracker bread (lahvosh) or other flatbread

1. In a medium skillet, cook onion, garlic, and oregano in hot olive oil until tender, stirring occasionally.

2. In a food processor bowl, combine onion mixture, beans, vinegar, and red pepper; cover and process until smooth, scraping the side of the container as necessary. Transfer to a serving dish. Serve with cracker bread or other flatbread. Makes about 1⅔ cups.

Make-Ahead Tip: Prepare White Bean Spread as directed. Cover and chill for up to 24 hours. Before serving, let stand at room temperature for 1 hour; stir.

Basil-Pepper Crostini
Prep: 15 minutes **Stand:** 30 minutes
Bake: 8 minutes

- ¼ cup thinly sliced red onion
- 1 clove garlic, minced
- 2 tablespoons olive oil
- 3 medium red and/or yellow sweet peppers, roasted*
- 4 teaspoons white or regular balsamic vinegar
- 1 tablespoon snipped fresh basil or ½ teaspoon dried basil, crushed

Dash salt
Dash ground black pepper
- 1 8-ounce loaf baguette-style French bread

Fresh basil leaves (optional)

1. In a large skillet, cook onion and garlic in hot olive oil until onion is tender, stirring occasionally. Remove from heat.

2. Cut peppers into thin strips. Add pepper strips, balsamic vinegar, snipped or dried basil, salt, and black pepper to onion mixture. Toss gently to mix. To blend flavors, let stand at room temperature for 30 minutes to 2 hours.

3. For toasts, cut bread into ½-inch-thick slices. Arrange slices on an ungreased baking sheet. Bake in a 425°F oven about 8 minutes or until crisp and light brown, turning once.

4. To assemble, top each piece of toast with a basil leaf, if desired, and about *1 tablespoon* of the pepper topping. Makes about 20 servings.

Make-Ahead Tip: Prepare Basil-Pepper Crostini as directed through step 3. Place topping and toasts in separate airtight containers. Chill for up to 24 hours. Before serving, let stand at room temperature for 30 minutes. Continue as directed in step 4.

*Note: To roast peppers, line a baking sheet with foil; set aside. Quarter sweet peppers; remove stems, seeds, and membranes. Place pepper pieces, skin sides up, on the prepared baking sheet. Bake in a 425°F oven for 20 to 25 minutes or until skins are blistered and dark. Wrap peppers in the foil; let stand for 15 minutes. Using a sharp knife, peel skins from peppers; discard skins.

Tomato-Eggplant Relish
Caponata (KAP-oh-NAH-tah)
Prep: 20 minutes **Cook:** 30 minutes

- 3 tablespoons olive oil
- 1 large eggplant, cut into ½-inch cubes (6 cups)
- 1 large onion, chopped (1 cup)
- 2 stalks celery, chopped (½ cup)
- ¼ cup red wine vinegar
- 2 tablespoons sugar
- ½ teaspoon salt*
- ½ teaspoon ground black pepper
- 2 large tomatoes, seeded and chopped (2 cups), or one 14½-ounce can diced tomatoes,* drained
- ⅓ cup chopped pitted green olives
- 1 3½-ounce jar capers, drained (¼ cup)
- ¼ cup canned tomato sauce
- ¼ cup pine nuts, toasted

1. In a large skillet, heat *2 tablespoons* of the olive oil over medium heat. Add eggplant; cook and stir for 5 to 6 minutes or until eggplant just starts to brown. Remove from skillet.

2. Add remaining oil to skillet; cook onion and celery in hot oil until tender, stirring occasionally.

3. Meanwhile, in small saucepan, combine vinegar, sugar, salt, and pepper. Cook and stir over medium-low heat until sugar is dissolved.

4. Add eggplant, tomatoes, olives, capers, tomato sauce, and pine nuts to onion mixture. Add vinegar mixture. Bring to boiling; reduce heat. Cover and simmer about 30 minutes or until vegetables are tender and sauce is thickened. Makes 10 to 12 servings.

*Note: If using canned tomatoes, omit salt.

> **Perhaps you've heard of ratatouille,** that tomato-eggplant relish so popular in the South of France? Well, *caponata* is its Sicilian cousin. Like ratatouille, this relish starts with eggplants, tomatoes, and onions—and the remaining ingredients vary with the cook. Serve *caponata* as a robust relish on an antipasto tray or as a side dish. Keep in mind that it tastes best served at room temperature.

Basil-Olive Spread
Tapenade (TAH-puh-nahd)
Start to finish: 15 minutes

- ¾ cup pitted green olives
- ¾ cup pitted kalamata olives or ripe olives
- 1 tablespoon olive oil
- 1 to 2 tablespoons dry red wine or chicken broth
- ¼ cup lightly packed fresh basil leaves
- 1 tablespoon Dijon-style mustard
- 1 clove garlic, minced
- ⅛ teaspoon ground black pepper
- ¾ cup finely chopped, seeded tomato
- 2 tablespoons thinly sliced green onion
- Fresh basil sprigs (optional)
- Toasted baguette slices

1. In a blender container or food processor bowl, combine olives, olive oil, wine, the ¼ cup basil, the mustard, garlic, and pepper. Cover; blend or process until finely chopped, scraping down side of container as necessary. (If using a blender, start at lowest speed.)

2. Transfer mixture to a serving bowl. Stir in tomato and green onion. If desired, garnish with basil sprigs. Serve with toasted baguette slices. Makes 1½ cups.

Make-Ahead Tip: Prepare Basil-Olive Spread as directed. Cover and chill for up to 8 hours. Before serving, let stand at room temperature for 30 minutes; stir.

Tapenade, **a paste made with black olives,** is a specialty of the South of France. While the traditional recipes include capers and anchovies in the mix, there are many variations on the theme. Green olives add a sprightly flavor, while a little tomato and green onion contribute color and texture. If you have any leftover *tapenade,* try it as a relish for broiled fish or roasted meats.

Garlic-Potato Dip
Skordalia (skor-dahl-YAH)
Prep: 20 minutes Cook: 15 minutes

- 1 pound baking potatoes, peeled and cut into 1-inch chunks (3 cups)
- 4 teaspoons bottled minced garlic
- ½ teaspoon salt
- 3 tablespoons lemon juice
- ½ cup olive oil
- Snipped fresh chives (optional)
- Pita wedges

1. In a medium saucepan, cook potatoes in enough boiling lightly salted water to cover about 15 minutes or until potatoes are very tender.

2. Meanwhile, using a mortar and pestle, mash the garlic with salt.

3. Drain potatoes; transfer to a food mill or potato ricer. Force potatoes through the mill or ricer into a medium bowl.

4. Beat potatoes and lemon juice with an electric mixer on high speed until smooth. Gradually add the olive oil, beating on low speed until mixture is very smooth. Beat in garlic paste just until combined. If desired, garnish with chives. Serve with pita wedges. Makes 2¼ cups.

Roasted Garlic
Prep: 10 minutes Bake: 25 minutes

- 4 medium heads garlic
- ¼ cup olive oil
- Toasted baguette slices

1. Peel away the dry outer leaves from each head of garlic, leaving skin on garlic cloves intact. Using a knife, cut about ¼ inch from the pointed top portion of each head, leaving the bulb intact but exposing individual cloves.

2. Place garlic heads, cut sides up, in a small baking dish; drizzle with oil. Bake, covered, in a 425°F oven for 25 to 35 minutes or until cloves feel soft when pressed. Cool slightly.

3. Press garlic pulp from individual cloves; mash pulp with a fork. Serve with toasted baguette slices. Makes ¼ cup.

Sesame-Chickpea Spread
Hummus bi Tahina
(HOOM-uhs bee tah-HEE-nah)

Start to finish: 15 minutes

1   15-ounce can chickpeas (garbanzo
    beans), rinsed and drained
¼   cup tahini (sesame seed paste) or
    3 tablespoons creamy peanut butter
    plus 1 tablespoon sesame oil
½   teaspoon finely shredded lemon peel
3   tablespoons lemon juice
1   tablespoon olive oil or cooking oil
2   cloves garlic, minced
¼   teaspoon salt
Dash cayenne pepper
Paprika (optional)
Pita bread wedges, party breads, or crackers

1. In a blender container or food processor bowl, combine chickpeas, tahini, lemon peel, lemon juice, oil, garlic, salt, and cayenne pepper. Cover; blend or process until smooth, scraping side of container as necessary.

2. Transfer spread to a serving dish. If desired, sprinkle with paprika. Serve with pita bread wedges, party breads, or crackers. Makes 1½ cups.

Make-Ahead Tip: Prepare Sesame-Chickpea Spread as directed through step 1. Transfer to an airtight storage container. Cover and store in the refrigerator for up to 1 week. Stir before serving.

Basil-Olive Spread, Sesame-Chickpea Spread, and Garlic-Potato Dip

Think Mediterranean cuisine, and foods such as olives, lemons, garlic, and fresh herbs spring to mind. This trio of spreads showcases all of those ingredients, served in traditional, yet surprisingly contemporary ways. The Greek potato spread offers a bracing dose of garlic. Mideastern hummus surprises with a breathy hint of lemon. And the French tapenade is profoundly based on olive oil and two kinds of olives, liberally seasoned with garlic and herbs.

Cozy Breakfasts & Brunches

WE'VE BORROWED some great ideas from other cultures that translate well to our beloved American breakfast and brunch traditions. Here, you'll find comforting and familiar foods—such as omelets, quiches, and Belgian waffles—dressed up with a little something special. You'll also discover lesser-known gems (including the Spanish version of French toast and a German pancake that's anything but flat). So, if you're looking for a cozy Christmas breakfast for the family or a knockout New Year's Day brunch for a houseful, the inspiration is right here.

Belgian Waffles (recipe, page 65)

Sherried French Toast
Torrijas (*tohr-REE-hahs*)
Prep: 10 minutes Cook: 4 minutes per batch

- 4 eggs
- 1 cup milk
- 2 tablespoons sugar
- 2 tablespoons dry sherry or orange juice
- ½ teaspoon ground cinnamon
- ½ teaspoon finely shredded orange peel (optional)
- 8 ½-inch-thick slices French bread
- 2 tablespoons butter
- 1 recipe Sherry Syrup (below) or maple syrup, warmed

1. In a shallow bowl, use a whisk or fork to beat eggs; beat in milk, sugar, sherry or orange juice, cinnamon, and, if desired, orange peel. Dip bread slices into egg mixture, coating both sides.

2. In a large skillet or on a griddle, melt *1 tablespoon* of the butter over medium heat. Add *half* of the bread slices; cook for 4 to 6 minutes or until golden, turning once. Repeat with remaining butter and bread slices.

3. Serve French toast warm with Sherry Syrup or maple syrup. Makes 4 servings.

Sherry Syrup: In a small saucepan, stir together 1 cup sugar, ½ cup water, and one 3-inch-long strip orange peel. Bring to boiling; reduce heat. Simmer, uncovered, for 10 minutes. Remove from heat. Stir in 2 tablespoons dry sherry or frozen orange juice concentrate, thawed.

> **We call it French toast,** the English call it "eggy bread," and the French call it *pain perdu*—which literally means "lost bread," referring to its origin as a way to use day-old bread. The Spaniards also have a take on the concept, known as *torrijas*. Sometimes it's a honey-drenched bread served as dessert, but here it makes a good twist on the ever-popular breakfast entrée.

Thyme-Mushroom Omelets
Start to finish: 25 minutes

- ¼ cup butter
- 1 cup sliced fresh mushrooms
- ½ cup sliced fresh or frozen pea pods, thawed
- 2 green onions, sliced
- 1½ teaspoons snipped fresh thyme or ¼ teaspoon dried thyme, crushed
- 4 eggs
- ¼ cup water
- ¼ teaspoon salt
- ⅛ teaspoon ground black pepper
- 2 ounces Gruyère or Swiss cheese, shredded (½ cup)

1. For filling, in a small skillet, melt *2 tablespoons* of the butter over medium heat; add mushrooms, pea pods, green onion, and thyme. Cook until mushrooms and pea pods are tender, stirring occasionally.

2. Meanwhile, for omelets, in a small bowl, use a whisk or fork to beat eggs; beat in water, salt, and pepper until combined but not frothy.

3. Heat an 8-inch nonstick skillet with flared sides over medium-high heat until skillet is hot. Add *1 tablespoon* of the remaining butter to skillet. When butter is melted, add *half* of the egg mixture to skillet; reduce heat to medium. Immediately begin stirring eggs gently but continuously with a wooden spatula until mixture resembles small pieces of cooked egg surrounded by liquid egg. Stop stirring. Cook for 30 to 60 seconds more or until egg is set but shiny.

4. Spoon *half* of the mushroom filling across the center of omelet. Sprinkle with *half* of the cheese. Using a spatula, lift and fold unfilled half of omelet over filling. Remove from heat. Transfer to a warm plate.

5. Keep omelet warm while making another omelet with remaining butter, eggs, filling, and cheese. Makes 2 servings.

Quiche originated in the Alsace-Lorraine region of northeastern France. The most famous version is quiche Lorraine (a recipe with bacon bits and sometimes cheese), but cooks everywhere have taken the egg pie and run with it in a world of ways. On your holiday brunch table, pair it with a tartly dressed green salad and French bread.

Dilled Salmon Quiche

Prep: 25 minutes Bake: 47 minutes
Stand: 10 minutes

- ½ of a 15-ounce package (1 crust) folded refrigerated unbaked piecrust
- 3 eggs
- ¾ cup dairy sour cream
- 2 ounces Gruyère or Swiss cheese, shredded (½ cup)
- ¼ cup mayonnaise or salad dressing
- 1 tablespoon snipped fresh dill or 1 teaspoon dried dill weed
- ¼ teaspoon ground black pepper
- 1 14¾-ounce can salmon, drained, flaked, and skin and bones removed

Fresh dill sprigs (optional)

1. Unfold pastry into a 9-inch pie plate. Trim; crimp edge as desired. Line unpricked pastry with a double thickness of foil. Bake in a 450°F oven for 8 minutes. Remove foil. Bake for 4 to 5 minutes more or until set and dry. Remove from oven. Reduce oven temperature to 325°F.

2. Meanwhile, for filling, in a bowl, use a fork to beat eggs; beat in sour cream, cheese, mayonnaise, dill, and pepper. Stir in salmon.

3. Pour filling into hot, baked pastry shell. Bake in the 325°F oven for 35 to 40 minutes or until knife inserted in center comes out clean. Let stand for 10 minutes before serving. If desired, garnish with dill sprigs. Makes 6 servings.

Spinach and Asiago Cheese Frittata
Prep: 15 minutes Bake: 13 minutes

- 1 leek, thinly sliced
- 2 cloves garlic, minced
- 1 tablespoon olive oil or cooking oil
- 4 cups torn fresh spinach
- 1 medium red sweet pepper, roasted (see note, page 57), or ⅔ cup bottled roasted red sweet pepper
- 3 ounces Asiago cheese, shredded (¾ cup)
- 1½ teaspoons snipped fresh thyme or ¼ teaspoon dried thyme, crushed
- ⅛ teaspoon salt
- ⅛ teaspoon ground black pepper
- 6 eggs, slightly beaten

1. Preheat oven to 350°F. In a 10-inch ovenproof skillet, cook leek and garlic in hot oil until tender, stirring often. Add spinach; cook and stir about 1 minute or until spinach is limp. Remove from heat.

2. Slice roasted pepper into strips. Stir pepper strips, ½ *cup* of the cheese, thyme, salt, and black pepper into skillet. Add eggs; stir to mix.

3. Bake for 13 to 15 minutes or until a knife inserted near the center comes out clean.

4. Top frittata with remaining cheese. To serve, loosen with a spatula; cut frittata into six wedges. Makes 6 servings.

Spinach and Asiago Cheese Frittata

Whenever you see the word *frittata,* think "Italian-style omelet"—but think "easy," too. Because flavorful ingredients are mixed with the eggs (rather than made as a filling), and because you cut the frittata into wedges (instead of folding it), you might find it easier to make than an omelet. Serve it as Italians would, with juicy wedges of fresh melon.

Waffles rank among Belgium's and Holland's best-known foods. In fact, they're often served as a snack in casual cafés or hot off the cart from street vendors. Belgian waffles, made with a yeast batter, are a little thicker than the standard waffle. Our waffles, crowned with warm lingonberry or lemon sauce, make heartwarming holiday breakfast treats for your family.

Belgian Waffles

Pictured on page 61.
Prep: 15 minutes Stand: 30 minutes
Bake: per waffle baker directions

  2 cups warm milk (105°F to 115°F)
  1 package active dry yeast
  4 egg yolks
  3 cups all-purpose flour
  ¼ cup sugar
  ½ teaspoon salt
  ½ cup butter, melted
  4 egg whites
Lingonberry or cherry preserves or maple
      syrup, warmed

1. In a large bowl, combine milk and yeast; stir until yeast is dissolved. Stir in egg yolks. In a medium bowl, stir together flour, sugar, and salt. Add the flour mixture to the milk mixture. Stir in butter; set aside.

2. In another medium bowl, beat egg whites with an electric mixer on medium to high speed until stiff peaks form (tips stand straight). Gently fold beaten egg whites into butter mixture, leaving a few puffs of egg white. Do not overmix. Let stand at room temperature for 30 minutes.

3. Pour ¾ *cup* to 1½ *cups* of the batter onto grids of a preheated, lightly greased waffle baker. Close lid quickly; do not open until done. Bake waffle according to manufacturer's directions. When done, use a fork to lift waffle off grid. Repeat with remaining batter.

4. Keep waffles warm while making other waffles. Serve waffles warm with lingonberry preserves. Makes 7 or 8 Belgian waffles or 12 to 14 (4-inch) waffles.

Gingerbread Waffles

Prep: 15 minutes
Bake: per waffle baker directions

  1¼ cups all-purpose flour
  1 teaspoon ground ginger
  ¾ teaspoon baking soda
  ½ teaspoon ground cinnamon
  ¼ teaspoon ground cloves
  ⅓ cup sugar
  ¼ cup shortening
  1 egg
  ½ cup milk
  ½ cup mild-flavored molasses
  1 recipe Lemon Sauce (recipe, page 66) or
      maple syrup, warmed

1. In a medium bowl, stir together flour, ginger, baking soda, cinnamon, and cloves. Make a well in the center; set aside.

2. In a small bowl, combine sugar and shortening; beat with an electric mixer on medium speed until fluffy. Add egg, milk, and molasses; beat until combined. Add all at once to flour mixture. Using a wooden spoon, stir just until moistened (batter should be slightly lumpy).

3. Pour 1 *cup* of the batter onto grids of a preheated, lightly greased waffle baker. Close lid quickly; do not open until done. Bake waffle according to manufacturer's directions. When done, use a fork to lift waffle off grid. Repeat with remaining batter.

4. Keep waffles warm while making other waffles. Serve warm with Lemon Sauce. Makes 8 (4-inch) waffles.

Puffed Apple Pancake

Apfelpfannkuchen literally means "apple-pan-cake." However, the term "flat as pancake" just doesn't apply to this traditional German treat. As it bakes in the oven, the eggy batter rises up and around the center for a puffy delight. Although it's impressive, there's nothing tricky about the dish at all—just be ready to quickly serve it hot, while it's still puffy.

Puffed Apple Pancake
Apfelpfannkuchen (ap-fel-phan-KOO-ken)
Prep: 15 minutes Bake: 18 minutes

    3   eggs
    ½   cup all-purpose flour
    ½   cup milk
    4   tablespoons butter, melted
    ¼   teaspoon salt
    ⅓   cup packed brown sugar
    2   medium cooking apples, peeled, cored,
        and sliced (2 cups)
    ¼   teaspoon ground cinnamon
    ¼   teaspoon ground nutmeg
    Sifted powdered sugar

1. Preheat oven to 450°F. In a medium bowl, use a whisk to beat eggs until frothy. Beat in flour, milk, *1 tablespoon* of the melted butter, and the salt until smooth.

2. Heat an 8×1½-inch round baking pan or ovenproof skillet in oven for 2 minutes. Add *1 tablespoon* melted butter; swirl pan to coat sides.

3. Immediately pour batter into hot pan. Bake for 18 to 20 minutes or until puffed and golden.

4. Meanwhile, for filling, in a medium skillet, stir brown sugar into remaining *2 tablespoons* melted butter until combined. Stir in apple slices, cinnamon, and nutmeg. Cook, uncovered, over medium heat for 3 to 5 minutes or until apples are crisp-tender, stirring occasionally.

5. Serve pancake immediately. (It will collapse as it cools.) To serve, spoon some of the filling into the center of the pancake. Sprinkle edge with powdered sugar. Cut into six wedges. Pass the remaining filling. Makes 6 servings.

Spiced Pancake Squares
Pannukakku (pah-noo-KAH-koo)
Prep: 15 minutes Bake: 25 minutes

    ¼   cup butter, melted
    5   eggs
    1½ cups milk
    1   cup all-purpose flour
    ½   cup sugar
    ½   teaspoon finely shredded lemon peel
    ¼   teaspoon salt
    ¼   teaspoon ground cardamom or ground
        allspice
    Sifted powdered sugar (optional)
    1   recipe Lemon Sauce (below) or maple
        syrup, warmed

1. Preheat oven to 400°F. Pour butter into a 13×9×2-inch baking pan; swirl to coat. Set aside.

2. In a large bowl, use a fork to beat eggs. Beat in milk, flour, sugar, peel, and salt until smooth.

3. Pour batter into the prepared pan. Sprinkle with cardamom. Bake about 25 minutes or until puffed and golden.

4. To serve, sprinkle pancake with powdered sugar, if desired. Cut into eight squares. Serve warm with Lemon Sauce. Makes 8 servings.

Lemon Sauce: In a small saucepan, stir together ⅔ cup sugar, ¼ cup water, 4 teaspoons cornstarch, 2 teaspoons finely shredded lemon peel, and ¼ cup lemon juice. Cook and stir over medium heat until mixture is slightly thickened and bubbly. Cook and stir for 1 minute more. Gradually stir hot mixture into 2 beaten egg yolks; return to pan. Cook and stir for 2 minutes more. Gradually stir in 6 tablespoons cut-up butter until melted. Stir in ¼ cup half-and-half, light cream, or milk.

Walnut-Cinnamon Pancake Stacks

Palacsinta (pah-lah-CHEN-tah)

Prep: 35 minutes   Bake: 10 minutes

- ½ **cup sugar**
- ¼ **cup ground walnuts**
- 1 **teaspoon ground cinnamon**
- ¼ **cup butter, softened**
- ¼ **teaspoon salt**
- 5 **egg yolks**
- ¾ **cup all-purpose flour**
- ⅓ **cup milk**
- ½ **teaspoon vanilla**
- 5 **egg whites**

1. In a small bowl, combine ¼ *cup* of the sugar, the walnuts, and cinnamon; set aside.

2. In a large bowl, combine remaining ¼ *cup* sugar, the butter, and salt; beat with an electric mixer on medium speed until mixed. Add egg yolks; beat well. Beat in flour. Add milk and vanilla; beat until mixed.

3. Wash beaters thoroughly. In another large bowl, beat egg whites with an electric mixer on medium to high speed until soft peaks form (tips curl). Fold egg whites into batter, leaving a few puffs of egg white. Do not overmix.

4. Heat a lightly greased griddle or heavy skillet over medium heat until a few drops of water dance across surface.

5. For each pancake, pour or spread a scant ¼ *cup* batter into a 4-inch circle on hot griddle. Cook over medium heat about 1 minute on each side or until golden, turning to cook second sides when surfaces are bubbly and edges are slightly dry. If pancakes brown too quickly, reduce heat to medium-low.

6. On a foil-lined baking sheet, stack *four* pancakes, sprinkling *1½ teaspoons* of the walnut mixture onto each pancake. Repeat with remaining pancakes and walnut mixture to make four stacks of four pancakes each.

7. Heat pancakes, uncovered, in a 300°F oven about 10 minutes or until heated through. To serve, cut into four wedges. Makes 4 servings.

Walnut-Cinnamon Pancake Stack

Crumpets
Prep: 20 minutes   Rise: 45 minutes
Cook: 4 minutes per batch

- 4   cups all-purpose flour
- 1   package active dry yeast
- ¼   teaspoon baking soda
- 3   cups milk
- 1   tablespoon sugar
- 1½ teaspoons salt

1. In a large bowl, stir together *3 cups* of the flour, the yeast, and baking soda; set aside.

2. In a medium saucepan, heat and stir milk, sugar, and salt just until warm (120°F to 130°F). Using a wooden spoon, stir into flour mixture. Stir in remaining flour. Cover; let rise in a warm place until double (about 45 minutes).

3. Heat a lightly greased griddle or heavy skillet over medium heat until a few drops of water dance across surface.

4. For each crumpet, spoon about *¼ cup* of the batter into a 3-inch circle on hot griddle. Cook over medium heat about 2 minutes on each side or until golden, turning to cook second sides when surfaces are bubbly and edges are slightly dry. If desired, toast crumpets. Serve warm. Makes about 22 crumpets.

Make-Ahead Tip: Prepare Crumpets as directed. Place in freezer bags; freeze for up to 1 month. Thaw at room temperature. Toast crumpets, if desired.

A hearty English breakfast often includes crumpets. These spongy bread rounds are cooked on a griddle, like pancakes, only they're more like English muffins in texture because they're made from a yeast batter. Serve them along with other British breakfast foods such as scrambled eggs; bangers (known stateside as sausage); or rashers (strips of bacon); and a good, strong cup of English breakfast tea. It's a meal fit for a queen!

Almond Pastry Puffs
Vandbakkelse (vahn-BAHK-el-sah)
Prep: 40 minutes   Bake: 50 minutes

- ½   cup cold butter
- 1   cup all-purpose flour
- 2   to 3 tablespoons cold water
- 1   recipe Almond Topping (below)
- 1   recipe Powdered Sugar Icing (below)
- ½   cup sliced almonds, toasted

1. For pastry, in a medium bowl, use a pastry blender to cut cold butter into flour until pieces are pea-size. Sprinkle *1 tablespoon* of the cold water over part of the mixture; gently toss with a fork. Push moistened dough to the side of the bowl. Repeat moistening flour mixture, using *1 tablespoon* of the water at a time, until all of the flour mixture is moistened. Form dough into a ball. Divide dough in half.

2. Lightly grease a large baking sheet; set aside. On a lightly floured surface, roll each dough portion into a 12×3-inch rectangle. Arrange rectangles 4 inches apart on prepared baking sheet. Evenly spread *half* of the Almond Topping onto each rectangle to about ½ inch from edges.

3. Bake in a 350°F oven for 50 to 55 minutes or until topping is golden. Cut diagonally into 1-inch-wide strips. Carefully transfer pastry strips to a wire rack to cool. (The topping will fall slightly, forming the custardy top of the puff.)

4. Drizzle icing onto pastry strips. Top with almonds. Makes about 20 servings.

Almond Topping: In a medium saucepan, combine 1 cup water and ½ cup cut-up butter; bring to boiling. Remove from heat; immediately stir in 1 teaspoon almond extract. Stir in 1 cup all-purpose flour. Return to heat. Stir vigorously over low heat about 1 minute or until dough forms a ball. Remove from heat; cool 5 minutes. Add 3 eggs, *one* at a time, beating with a wooden spoon after each until smooth and glossy.

Powdered Sugar Icing: In a small bowl, stir together 1 cup sifted powdered sugar and 1 tablespoon milk. Stir in enough additional milk, 1 teaspoon at a time, to make an icing of drizzling consistency.

Make-Ahead Tip: Prepare Almond Pastry Puffs as directed. Cover; chill up to 3 days.

Are Danish pastries really Danish? Well, yes and no. When Danish journeymen bakers went on strike in the mid-19th century, they were replaced for a time by Austrian bakers. The Austrians introduced the idea of layering fat with yeast dough—the process that gives today's Danish pastries their hallmark flakiness. After the Austrian bakers went home, the Danish bakers put their own spin on the dough, and the rest is sweet-treat history!

Raspberry Danish Pastry
Prep: 15 minutes Bake: 15 minutes

- ½ of a 17.3-ounce package (1 sheet) frozen puff pastry sheets, thawed
- ⅓ cup seedless raspberry preserves
- 1 recipe Almond Glaze (right)

1. On a lightly floured surface, unfold puff pastry. If necessary, use a rolling pin to smooth the pastry. Cut into 12 strips. Wrapping loosely, coil each strip into a spiral. Moisten outside end of each strip with water; secure to the pastry spiral to prevent uncoiling during baking.

2. Arrange pastries on an ungreased baking sheet. Bake in a 400°F oven about 15 minutes or until golden. Remove from baking sheet; cool on a wire rack.

3. Before serving, in a small saucepan, heat preserves until melted, stirring often. Drizzle warm preserves and Almond Glaze over pastries. Makes 12 pastries.

Almond Glaze: In a small bowl, stir together 1 cup sifted powdered sugar and ½ teaspoon almond extract. Add enough milk (2 to 3 teaspoons) to make a glaze of drizzling consistency.

Heritage Holiday Breads

IN THE OLD WORLD, bread bakers had a knack for adding a touch of holiday magic when creating the staff of life. In our bountiful basket, you'll discover traditions to add meaning to your holidays. Wish your family good luck and prosperity with Czech *Kolackys*. Honor the birth of Christ with Germany's *Christstollen*, folded to resemble the baby wrapped in swaddling clothes. Or celebrate light during the dark days of winter with Swedish *St. Lucia Buns*. Share our sweet and savory loaves and their symbolism at meals or coffee-and-tea gatherings this holiday.

Cherry Tea Ring (recipe, page 72)

Cherry Tea Rings
Pictured on page 71.
Prep: 50 minutes Rise: 2 hours
Bake: 25 minutes

- 1½ cups milk
- ½ cup butter
- 2 packages active dry yeast
- 7 to 7½ cups all-purpose flour
- ½ cup sugar
- 2 eggs, slightly beaten
- 1½ teaspoons salt
- 2 cups snipped dried tart cherries
- 1 recipe Cinnamon Filling (right)
- 1 recipe Almond Glaze (right)

1. In a saucepan, heat and stir milk and butter over low heat just until warm and butter is almost melted. Cool to lukewarm (105°F to 115°F).

2. In a bowl, dissolve yeast in ½ cup *lukewarm water* (105°F to 115°F); let stand 5 minutes. Stir in milk mixture, 3½ *cups* flour, sugar, eggs, and salt. Stir in as much remaining flour as you can.

3. Turn onto a lightly floured surface. Knead in enough remaining flour to make a moderately stiff dough that is smooth and elastic (6 to 8 minutes total). Shape into a ball. Place in a lightly greased bowl; turn once. Cover; let rise in a warm place until double (about 1½ hours).

4. Meanwhile, bring 2 cups *water* to boiling; remove from heat. Add cherries; let stand 5 minutes. Drain; squeeze out excess water.

5. Punch down dough. Turn onto a floured surface. Divide in half. Cover; let rest 10 minutes. Meanwhile, grease a large baking sheet; set aside.

6. Roll each dough portion into a 15×9-inch rectangle. Spread each with Cinnamon Filling and cherries. Starting from a long side, roll up each into a spiral; seal seams.

7. Place each roll on prepared baking sheet. Attach ends to form two circles; pinch seams to seal. Using a sharp knife, cut slits from outside edges to centers, leaving about 1 inch attached at centers. Repeat at 1-inch intervals around ring. Gently turn each slice to show swirl. Cover; let rise until nearly double (about 30 minutes). Preheat oven to 350°F.

8. Bake about 25 minutes or until bread sounds hollow when tapped (the centers may be lighter in color). If necessary to prevent overbrowning, cover rings with foil for the last 5 to 10 minutes

of baking. Remove from baking sheet. Cool on a wire rack. Drizzle with Almond Glaze. Makes 2 rings (24 servings).

Cinnamon Filling: In a medium bowl, stir together ⅔ cup granulated sugar, ⅔ cup packed brown sugar, ⅓ cup all-purpose flour, and 1 tablespoon ground cinnamon. Using a pastry blender or fork, cut in ½ cup butter until crumbly.

Almond Glaze: In a small bowl, stir together 2½ cups sifted powdered sugar, 2 teaspoons light-colored corn syrup, and ½ teaspoon almond extract. Stir in enough milk (3 to 4 tablespoons) to make a glaze of drizzling consistency.

Orange-Rye Bread
Limpa (LIHM-pah)
Prep: 30 minutes Rise: 1¾ hours
Bake: 35 minutes

- 3½ to 4 cups all-purpose flour
- 2 packages active dry yeast
- ¼ cup sugar
- ¼ cup shortening
- ¼ cup molasses
- 1 teaspoon salt
- 4 teaspoons finely shredded orange peel
- 1½ cups rye flour

1. In a large bowl, stir together *2 cups* of the all-purpose flour and the yeast; set aside.

2. In a medium saucepan, heat and stir 1½ cups *water*, the sugar, shortening, molasses, and salt just until warm (120°F to 130°F) and shortening is almost melted. Add to flour mixture. Beat with an electric mixer on low to medium speed for 30 seconds. Beat on high speed for 3 minutes, scraping side of bowl. Using a wooden spoon, stir in orange peel, rye flour, and as much remaining all-purpose flour as you can.

3. Turn out dough onto a lightly floured surface. Knead in enough of the remaining all-purpose flour to make a moderately stiff dough that is smooth and elastic (6 to 8 minutes total). Shape dough into a ball. Place in a greased bowl; turn once to grease the surface. Cover; let rise in a warm place until double in size (1 to 1½ hours).

4. Punch down dough. Turn out dough onto a lightly floured surface. Divide dough in half. Cover; let rest for 10 minutes. Meanwhile, lightly grease a large baking sheet.

5. Shape into round loaves by gently pulling each portion into a ball, tucking edges under. Place on prepared baking sheet. Flatten each to a 5-inch round. Cover; let rise until nearly double (about 45 minutes). Preheat oven to 350°F.

6. Bake about 35 minutes or until bread sounds hollow when tapped. If necessary to prevent overbrowning, cover loosely with foil the last 10 minutes. Remove from baking sheet. Cool on a wire rack. Makes 2 loaves (16 to 20 servings).

St. Lucia Buns
Lussekake (loo-suh-KAWK-ker)
Prep: 45 minutes Rise: 1½ hours
Bake: 12 minutes

> 2½ to 3 cups all-purpose flour
> 1 package active dry yeast
> ¾ cup milk
> ⅓ cup granulated sugar
> ¼ cup butter
> ½ teaspoon salt
> ¼ teaspoon ground cardamom
> ⅛ teaspoon ground saffron
> 2 eggs
> ¼ cup golden raisins
> ¼ cup ground almonds
> Golden raisins
> 1 tablespoon water
> Coarse sugar

1. In a large bowl, stir together *1 cup* of the flour and the yeast; set aside.

2. In a small saucepan, heat and stir milk, granulated sugar, butter, salt, cardamom, and saffron just until warm (120°F to 130°F) and butter is almost melted. Add to flour mixture. Add *one* egg. Beat with an electric mixer on low to medium speed for 30 seconds. Beat on high for 3 minutes, scraping bowl constantly. Using a wooden spoon, stir in the ¼ cup raisins, almonds, and as much of the remaining flour as you can.

3. Turn out dough onto a lightly floured surface. Knead in enough of the remaining flour to make a moderately soft dough that is smooth and elastic (3 to 5 minutes total). Shape dough into a ball. Place in a lightly greased bowl; turn once to grease the surface. Cover; let rise in a warm place until double in size (1 to 1¼ hours).

St. Lucia Buns

December 13, St. Lucia's Day in Sweden, honors the saint known as the Queen of Light, and the celebrations bring lightheartedness to winter's dark days. The festivities kick off early that morning, when the family's eldest daughter, wearing a white dress and a crown of candles signifying light, awakens everyone with these saffron-infused sweet rolls and coffee.

4. Punch down dough. Turn out onto a lightly floured surface. Divide in half. Cover; let rest for 10 minutes. Meanwhile, grease a baking sheet.

5. Divide each portion into 12 pieces; roll into 12-inch-long ropes. Arrange ropes 3 inches apart on prepared sheet. Form each into an "S" shape, coiling the ends snail fashion. (If desired, make double buns by pressing centers of two S-shaped pieces together to form a cross, as shown above.) Press a raisin into the center of each coil. Cover; let rise until nearly double in size (30 to 40 minutes). Preheat oven to 350°F.

6. In a small bowl, stir together remaining egg and the water; lightly brush onto buns. Sprinkle with coarse sugar. Bake about 12 minutes or until golden. Remove from baking sheet. Serve warm, or cool on a wire rack. Makes 24 single buns.

Cardamom Bread Twist
Viipuri (vih-PUR-ree)
Prep: 30 minutes Rise: 1½ hours
Bake: 20 minutes

 4 to 4½ cups all-purpose flour
 1 package active dry yeast
 ½ to 1 teaspoon ground cardamom
 ¾ cup milk
 ½ cup sugar
 ⅓ cup butter
 ¼ cup water
 ½ teaspoon salt
 3 eggs
 Coarse sugar

1. In a large bowl, combine *2 cups* of the flour, the yeast, and cardamom; set aside.

2. In a medium saucepan, heat and stir milk, sugar, butter, water, and salt just until warm (120°F to 130°F) and butter is almost melted. Add milk mixture to flour mixture; add eggs. Beat with an electric mixer on low to medium speed for 30 seconds. Beat on high speed for 3 minutes, scraping bowl constantly. Using a wooden spoon, stir in as much of the remaining flour as you can.

3. Turn out dough onto a lightly floured surface. Knead in enough of the remaining flour to make a moderately soft dough that is smooth and elastic (3 to 5 minutes total). Shape dough into a ball. Place in a lightly greased bowl, turning once to grease the surface. Cover; let rise in a warm place until double (1 to 1¼ hours).

4. Punch down dough. Turn out onto a lightly floured surface. Divide into thirds. Cover; let rest for 10 minutes. Lightly grease a baking sheet.

5. Roll each portion into a 15-inch-long rope. On prepared baking sheet, form each rope into a circle, leaving ends extended 6 inches at bottoms. Holding ends of rope toward center of circles, twist together. Press ends together; tuck under center at top of circle, forming a pretzel shape. Cover; let rise in a warm place until nearly double in size (about 30 minutes). Preheat oven to 375°F.

6. Slightly beat remaining egg; brush onto loaf. Sprinkle with coarse sugar. Bake for 20 to 25 minutes or until bread sounds hollow when tapped. If necessary to prevent overbrowning, cover with foil for the last 10 minutes of baking. Remove from baking sheet. Cool on a wire rack. Makes 1 loaf (16 servings).

Citron Fruit Loaf
Julekake (yul-leh-KAWK-ker)
Prep: 30 minutes Rise: 2¾ hours
Bake: 40 minutes

 3¼ to 3½ cups all-purpose flour
 1 package active dry yeast
 ½ teaspoon ground cardamom
 1 cup milk
 ½ cup sugar
 ¼ cup butter
 ½ teaspoon salt
 1 egg
 ½ cup golden raisins
 ½ cup diced candied citron
 ½ cup diced mixed candied fruits and peels
 Sifted powdered sugar

1. In a large bowl, stir together *1½ cups* of the flour, the yeast, and cardamom; set aside.

2. In a small saucepan, heat and stir milk, sugar, butter, and salt just until warm (120°F to 130°F) and butter is almost melted. Add milk mixture to flour mixture; add egg. Beat with an electric mixer on low to medium speed for 30 seconds. Beat on high speed for 3 minutes, scraping bowl constantly. Using a wooden spoon, stir in as much of the remaining flour as you can. Stir in raisins, fruits and peels, and citron.

3. Turn out dough onto a lightly floured surface. Knead in enough of the remaining flour to make a moderately soft dough that is smooth and elastic (3 to 5 minutes total). Shape dough into a ball. Place in a lightly greased bowl; turn once to grease the surface. Cover; let rise in a warm place until double in size (about 1¾ hours).

4. Punch down dough. Turn out onto a lightly floured surface. Cover; let rest for 10 minutes. Meanwhile, lightly grease an 8×1½ inch round baking pan; set aside.

5. Shape into a round loaf by gently pulling into a ball, tucking edges under. Place in prepared pan; flatten to fill pan. Cover; let rise until nearly double (about 1 hour). Preheat oven to 350°F.

6. Bake for 40 to 45 minutes or until bread sounds hollow when tapped. If necessary to prevent overbrowning, cover loosely with foil for the last 10 minutes of baking. Remove from pan. Cool on a wire rack. Sprinkle with powdered sugar. Makes 1 loaf (12 servings).

Orange-Almond Braids

Vanocka (vah-NOK-kah)

Prep: 30 minutes Rise: 2½ hours
Bake: 30 minutes

>   7¾ to 8¼ cups all-purpose flour
>   2   packages active dry yeast
>   1   cup granulated sugar
>   1   cup milk
>   1   cup butter
>   2   teaspoons salt
>   7   eggs
>   2   tablespoons vanilla
>   1   cup raisins
>   1   cup finely chopped candied orange peel
>   1   cup chopped blanched almonds
>   1   teaspoon anise seeds, crushed
>   Coarse sugar
>   Sliced almonds

1. In a large bowl, combine *3½ cups* of the flour and the yeast; set aside.

2. In a small saucepan, heat and stir granulated sugar, milk, butter, and salt just until warm (120°F to 130°F) and butter is almost melted. Add to flour mixture. Add *six* eggs and the vanilla. Beat with an electric mixer on low for 30 seconds. Beat on high for 3 minutes, scraping bowl. Stir in raisins, peel, chopped almonds, anise seeds, and as much remaining flour as you can.

3. Turn out dough onto a lightly floured surface. Knead in enough remaining flour to make a moderately soft dough that is smooth (3 to 5 minutes total). Shape into a ball. Place in a greased very large bowl; turn once. Cover; let rise in a warm place until double (1½ to 2 hours).

4. Punch down. Divide in half. Cover; let rest 10 minutes. Grease two baking sheets; set aside.

5. Divide each half into three portions; roll into 18-inch-long ropes. For each braid, line up three ropes 1 inch apart on prepared baking sheet. Starting in center, bring left rope under center rope. Bring right rope under new center rope. Repeat to end. Braid from center on the other end, bringing outside ropes alternately over center rope. Seal ends. Cover; let rise until nearly double (1 to 1½ hours). Preheat oven to 350°F.

6. Beat remaining egg; brush onto loaves. Sprinkle with coarse sugar and sliced almonds. Bake about 30 minutes or until bread sounds hollow when tapped. To prevent overbrowning, cover loosely with foil for the last 10 minutes. Remove from baking sheet. Cool on a wire rack. Makes 2 braids (32 servings).

This sweet Czech Christmas bread was considered difficult to make in times past. Hence, curious customs arose to ensure a successful loaf: for example, the cook was to wear a white apron and a kerchief—and not speak—while mixing the dough and had to jump up and down as the dough rose. Happily, our Test Kitchen simplified the recipe, so you don't have to wear white and hop around your kitchen.

Orange-Almond Braid

Walnut Swirl Bread
Babovka (BAH-bahv-kah)
Prep: 30 minutes Rise: 2¼ hours
Bake: 35 minutes

- 1 package active dry yeast
- ¼ cup warm water (105°F to 115°F)
- 2 eggs
- ¼ cup sugar
- 3¼ to 3¾ cups all-purpose flour
- ½ cup milk
- ¼ cup butter, softened
- ½ teaspoon salt
- ½ teaspoon ground mace or nutmeg
- ½ teaspoon finely shredded lemon peel
- 2 tablespoons butter, melted
- 1 recipe Spiced Walnut Filling (right)
- 1 recipe Vanilla Icing (right)

Walnut Swirl Bread

This sweet coffeecake is based on a recipe for *potica*, a traditional Christmastime treat from Eastern Europe. Often, the dough was rolled and stretched thin—a somewhat tricky process—so that it could bring a multitude of delicate layers to the spiraled treat. Our simplified version still brings all the sweet, nutty goodness, but with a lot more ease.

1. In a small bowl, dissolve the yeast in the warm water; let stand for 5 minutes.

2. In a large bowl, beat eggs and sugar with an electric mixer on medium speed until combined. Add *1 cup* of the flour, the milk, the ¼ cup butter, the salt, mace, and lemon peel; beat until combined. Beat in the yeast mixture. Using a wooden spoon, stir in as much of the remaining flour as you can.

3. Turn out dough onto lightly floured surface. Knead in enough of the remaining flour to make a moderately soft dough that is smooth and elastic (3 to 5 minutes total). Shape dough into a ball. Place in a lightly greased bowl; turn once to grease the surface. Cover; let rise in a warm place until double in size (about 1½ hours).

4. Punch down dough. Turn out dough onto a lightly floured surface. Cover and let rest for 10 minutes. Meanwhile, lightly grease a baking sheet; set aside.

5. Roll dough into a 12×8-inch rectangle. Brush with melted butter; sprinkle with Spiced Walnut Filling. Starting from a long side, roll up into a spiral. Pinch ends and seams to seal. Place, seam side down, on prepared baking sheet; shape into a crescent. Cover; let rise in warm place until nearly double in size (about 45 minutes). Preheat oven to 350°F.

6. Bake for 35 to 40 minutes or until bread sounds hollow when tapped. If necessary to prevent overbrowning, cover loosely with foil for the last 10 minutes of baking. Remove from baking sheet. Cool on a wire rack. Drizzle with Powdered Sugar Icing. Makes 1 loaf (16 servings).

Spiced Walnut Filling: In a small bowl, stir together ¾ cup sugar, ½ cup finely chopped walnuts, ½ cup raisins, 2 tablespoons rum, and 1 teaspoon ground cinnamon.

Vanilla Icing: In a small bowl, stir together 1 cup sifted powdered sugar, 1 tablespoon milk, and ¼ teaspoon vanilla. Stir in enough additional milk, ½ teaspoon at a time, to make icing of drizzling consistency.

Make-Ahead Tip: Prepare Walnut Swirl Bread as directed. Wrap cooled bread in foil or plastic wrap. Store at room temperature for up to 3 days. (Or place cooled bread in a freezer bag; freeze for up to 2 months.)

Fruit-Filled Buns
Kolackys (koh-LAH-cheez)

Prep: 30 minutes **Rise:** 1½ hours
Bake: 10 minutes

      3¾ to 4¼ cups all-purpose flour
      1   package active dry yeast
      1   cup milk
      ¾   cup butter
      ½   cup sugar
      ½   teaspoon salt
      4   egg yolks
      1   teaspoon finely shredded lemon peel
      1   recipe Apricot, Cherry, or Plum Filling
          (right), or canned poppy seed or other
          cake and pastry filling
      2   tablespoons butter, melted

1. In a large bowl, stir together *2 cups* of the flour and the yeast; set aside.

2. In a medium saucepan, heat and stir milk, the ¾ cup butter, the sugar, and salt just until warm (120°F to 130°F) and butter is almost melted. Add to flour mixture. Add egg yolks. Beat with an electric mixer on low speed for 30 seconds. Beat on high for 3 minutes, scraping bowl. Using a wooden spoon, stir in lemon peel and as much remaining flour as you can.

3. Turn out dough onto a lightly floured surface. Knead in enough remaining flour to make a moderately soft dough that is smooth and elastic (3 to 5 minutes total). Shape into a ball. Place in a greased bowl; turn once. Cover; let rise in a warm place until double (1 to 1½ hours).

4. Punch down dough. Turn out dough onto a lightly floured surface. Divide dough in half. Cover; let rest for 10 minutes. Meanwhile, lightly grease a baking sheet; set aside.

5. Shape each portion of dough into 12 balls, gently pulling edges under. Arrange balls 3 inches apart on the prepared baking sheet. Slightly flatten each ball to a 2½-inch round. Cover; let rise until nearly double in size (about 30 minutes). Preheat oven to 375°F.

6. Using your thumb, make an indentation in the center of each dough circle. Spoon about *2 teaspoons* filling into each indentation. Lightly brush with the 2 tablespoons melted butter.

7. Bake for 10 to 12 minutes or until golden. Remove from baking sheet. Cool on a wire rack. Makes 24 rolls.

Apricot Filling: In a small saucepan, combine 1 cup snipped dried apricots and enough water to come 1 inch above the apricots. Bring to boiling; reduce heat. Cover and simmer for 10 to 15 minutes or until apricots are very soft. Drain, reserving 2 tablespoons cooking liquid. In a blender or food processor, combine apricots, the reserved cooking liquid, ¼ cup sugar, 1 teaspoon lemon juice, and ⅛ teaspoon ground nutmeg. Cover; blend or process until smooth, stopping to scrape side as necessary. Set aside to cool.

Cherry Filling: In a small bowl, gently stir together 1 cup canned cherry pie filling, ¼ teaspoon rum extract, and ⅛ teaspoon ground cardamom or allspice.

Plum Filling: In a medium saucepan combine 1 pound pitted dried plums (prunes) and ½ cup water. Bring to boiling; reduce heat. Cover and simmer for 10 minutes. Cool for 20 minutes; drain. Place drained plums in a food processor; cover and process until smooth, scraping side of container as necessary. Add ½ cup sugar, 1 teaspoon vanilla, ¼ teaspoon salt, and ¼ teaspoon ground cinnamon; cover and process until mixed.

Diamond Raisin Bread
Duivekater (dive-en-KAY-ter)
Prep: 30 minutes Rise: 1¾ hours
Bake: 30 minutes

   4 to 4½ cups all-purpose flour
   1 package active dry yeast
   1 cup milk
   ½ cup butter
   ⅓ cup sugar
   ½ teaspoon salt
   3 eggs
   1½ cups raisins
   1 cup chopped walnuts

1. In a large bowl, stir together *2 cups* of the flour and the yeast; set aside.

2. In a medium saucepan, heat and stir milk, butter, sugar, and salt just until warm (120°F to 130°F) and butter is almost melted. Add to flour mixture. Add *two* of the eggs. Beat with an electric mixer on low to medium speed for 30 seconds. Beat on high speed for 3 minutes, scraping bowl constantly. Using a wooden spoon, stir in raisins, walnuts, and as much of the remaining flour as you can.

3. Turn out dough onto a lightly floured surface. Knead in enough of the remaining flour to make a moderately soft dough that is smooth and elastic (3 to 5 minutes total). Shape into a ball. Place in a lightly greased bowl; turn once to grease the surface. Cover; let rise in a warm place until double in size (1 to 1½ hours).

4. Punch down dough. Turn out dough onto a lightly floured surface. Cover; let rest for 10 minutes. Meanwhile, grease a baking sheet.

5. On prepared baking sheet, shape dough into a 12×8-inch diamond, measuring from point to point. Using a sharp knife, cut about two-thirds of the way from the center to each corner. Spread cut slightly so edges are about ¼ inch apart. Cover; let rise until nearly double in size (45 to 60 minutes). Preheat oven to 325°F.

6. Slightly beat remaining egg; brush onto loaf. Bake for 30 to 35 minutes or until bread sounds hollow when tapped. Remove bread from baking sheet. Cool on a wire rack. Makes 1 loaf (10 to 12 servings).

Pear-Fennel Bread
Hutzelbrot (HUT-sel-brawt)
Prep: 45 minutes Stand: 8 hours
Rise: 2 hours Bake: 40 minutes

   4 cups water
   2 cups dried pears (about 7 ounces)
   1 package active dry yeast
   ¼ cup lukewarm water (105°F to 115°F)
   5 to 5¼ cups all-purpose flour
   ½ teaspoon salt
   ⅛ teaspoon baking soda
   2 tablespoons lukewarm water
      (105°F to 115°F)
   ⅓ cup butter, softened
   ½ cup packed brown sugar
   1 egg
   1½ teaspoons fennel seeds, crushed
   1 teaspoon ground cinnamon
   1½ cups raisins
   1 tablespoon butter, melted

1. In a large saucepan, combine the 4 cups water and the dried pears. Bring to boiling; reduce heat. Cover and simmer about 20 minutes or until pears are very tender. Drain pears, reserving *1 cup* of the cooking liquid. Chop the pears; cover and refrigerate. Cool the reserved liquid to lukewarm (105°F to 115°F).

2. In a large bowl, dissolve yeast in the ¼ cup warm water; let stand for 5 minutes. Stir in the reserved pear liquid. Stir in 1½ *cups* of the flour. Cover; let stand for at least 8 hours or up to 24 hours at room temperature.

3. In a small bowl, stir together salt and baking soda; stir in the 2 tablespoons warm water. Stir into yeast mixture; set aside.

4. In a large bowl, beat butter with an electric mixer on low to medium speed for 30 seconds. Beat in brown sugar until combined. Beat in egg, fennel seeds, and cinnamon. Add yeast mixture; beat just until combined. Using a wooden spoon, stir in pears, raisins, and as much of the remaining flour as you can.

5. Turn out dough onto a lightly floured surface. Knead in enough of the remaining flour to make a moderately stiff dough that is smooth and elastic (6 to 8 minutes total). Shape dough into a ball. Place dough in a lightly greased bowl; turn once to grease surface. Cover; let rise in a warm place until double in size (1¼ to 1½ hours).

6. Punch down dough. Turn out dough onto a lightly floured surface. Divide dough in half. Cover; let rest for 10 minutes. Meanwhile, lightly grease two 8×4×2-inch loaf pans; set aside.

7. Shape dough by gently pulling each portion into a loaf, tucking edges under. Place loaves in the prepared loaf pans. Brush loaves with the melted butter. Cover; let rise in a warm place until nearly double in size (45 to 60 minutes). Preheat oven to 375°F.

8. Bake about 40 minutes or until bread sounds hollow when tapped. If necessary to prevent overbrowning, cover loosely with foil for the last 10 minutes of baking. Remove from pans. Cool on a wire rack. Makes 2 loaves (32 servings).

Almond Fruit Bread
Christstollen (krihs-STOH-luhn)
Prep: 30 minutes   Rise: 2¼ hours
Bake: 25 minutes

  4½ to 5 cups all-purpose flour
  2 packages active dry yeast
  1 teaspoon ground nutmeg
  1¼ cups milk
  ½ cup granulated sugar
  ½ cup butter
  ¾ teaspoon salt
  1 egg
  1 cup diced mixed candied fruits and peels
  ½ cup golden raisins
  ½ cup dried currants
  ¾ cup chopped almonds
  1 tablespoon finely shredded lemon peel
Milk
Sifted powdered sugar

1. In a large bowl, stir together *2 cups* of the flour, the yeast, and nutmeg; set aside.

2. In a medium saucepan, heat and stir the 1¼ cups milk, the granulated sugar, butter, and salt until warm (120°F to 130°F) and butter is almost melted. Add to flour mixture; add egg. Beat with an electric mixer on low to medium speed for 30 seconds. Beat on high speed for 3 minutes, scraping bowl constantly. Using a wooden spoon, stir in candied fruits and peels, raisins, currants, almonds, and lemon peel; stir in as much of the remaining flour as you can.

Almond Fruit Bread

Christstollen **has humble origins,** like the Christ child the bread is named for. The traditional folding of the dough is said to resemble the newborn child's swaddling clothes. The first recipes for this German specialty, dating back to 1400, called for water, oats, and flour, because baking with butter and milk was forbidden by religious beliefs. Today, stollen is a buttery-rich sweet bread, studded with fruits and almonds.

3. Turn out dough onto a lightly floured surface. Knead in enough of the remaining flour to make a moderately soft dough that is smooth and elastic (3 to 5 minutes total). Shape into a ball. Place in a lightly greased bowl; turn once to grease the surface. Cover; let rise in a warm place until double in size (1½ to 2 hours).

4. Punch down dough. Turn out dough onto a lightly floured surface. Divide dough into three portions. Cover and let rest for 10 minutes. Meanwhile, grease two large baking sheets.

5. Roll each dough portion into a 10×6-inch oval. For each oval, without stretching, fold a long side over to within 1 inch of opposite side; press edges lightly to seal. Place on prepared baking sheets. Cover; let rise until nearly double in size (45 to 60 minutes). Preheat oven to 350°F.

6. Brush loaves with additional milk. Bake for 25 to 30 minutes or until bread sounds hollow when tapped. For even baking, switch baking sheet positions halfway through baking. If necessary to prevent overbrowning, cover loosely with foil the last 5 minutes. Remove from baking sheets. Cool on a wire rack. Sprinkle with powdered sugar. Makes 3 loaves (30 servings).

Anise-Raisin Ring

In Italy, Christmas might not come without this fruit-and-citrus-studded brioche-style bread. Traditionally baked in a special *panettone* mold (a fluted tube pan also will do for this recipe), it's said to have been invented by mistake, when a baker named Toni botched a different bread recipe. The mistake soon became a hit, and people started asking for "Toni's bread"—which is, essentially, what *panettone* means. Why not do as the Italians—wrap up loaves in big boxes tied with festive bows for an irresistible holiday food gift?

Anise-Raisin Ring
Panettone (pan-uh-TOH-nee)
Stand: 20 minutes Prep: 30 minutes
Rise: 1¾ hours Bake: 35 minutes

    1   cup orange juice or water
    ½   cup chopped candied orange peel
        or citron
    1   cup golden and/or dark raisins
    3½ to 4 cups all-purpose flour
    1   package active dry yeast
    1   teaspoon anise seeds, crushed
    ½   cup milk
    ½   cup butter
    ¼   cup sugar
    ½   teaspoon salt
    3   eggs
    1   teaspoon finely shredded lemon peel
        (set aside)
    1   tablespoon lemon juice
    1   teaspoon vanilla
    1   recipe Vanilla Icing (recipe, page 76)
    Slivered citrus peel (optional)

1. In a small saucepan, bring orange juice to boiling; remove from heat. Stir in orange peel and raisins. Cover; let stand for 20 minutes.

2. Meanwhile, in a large bowl, stir together 1¾ cups flour, the yeast, and anise seeds; set aside.

3. In a medium saucepan, heat and stir milk, butter, sugar, and salt just until warm (120°F to 130°F) and butter is almost melted. Add to flour mixture. Add eggs, lemon juice, and vanilla. Beat with an electric mixer on low for 30 seconds. Beat on high for 3 minutes, scraping bowl. Drain fruit, discarding liquid. Stir in fruit, lemon peel, and as much remaining flour as you can.

4. Turn out dough onto a lightly floured surface. Knead in enough remaining flour to make a moderately soft dough that is smooth and elastic (3 to 5 minutes total). Shape into a ball. Place in a greased bowl; turn once. Cover; let rise in a warm place until double in size (about 1 hour).

5. Punch down dough. Turn out onto a floured surface. Cover; let rest for 10 minutes. Grease a 12-cup panettone pan or 10-inch fluted tube pan.

6. Make a 2-inch hole in center; place in pan. Cover; let rise in a warm place until nearly double in size (45 to 60 minutes). Preheat oven to 375°F.

7. Bake for 35 to 40 minutes or until a wooden toothpick inserted near center comes out clean

and bread sounds hollow when tapped. If necessary to prevent overbrowning, cover with foil the last 10 minutes. Remove from pan. Cool on a wire rack. Drizzle with Powdered Sugar Icing. If desired, sprinkle with slivered citrus peel. Makes 1 ring (12 servings).

Lemon-Raisin Loaves
Pao Doce (POW-doh-chee)
Prep: 45 minutes Rise: 1¾ hours
Bake: 35 minutes

    1   cup diced, peeled potato
    1   cup sugar
    ⅓   cup butter
    2   teaspoons salt
    6¾ to 7¼ cups all-purpose flour
    2   packages active dry yeast
    5   eggs
    2   cups raisins
    2   teaspoons finely shredded lemon peel

1. In a covered small saucepan, cook potato in 2 cups boiling *water* about 15 minutes or until tender. Drain, reserving 1⅔ cups cooking liquid. Mash potato. Add reserved liquid, sugar, butter, and salt; cool just until warm (120°F to 130°F).

2. In a bowl, combine 3 cups flour and the yeast. Add potato mixture and *four* eggs. Beat with an electric mixer on low speed for 30 seconds. Beat on high for 3 minutes, scraping bowl. Using a wooden spoon, stir in raisins, peel, and as much of the remaining flour as you can.

3. Turn out onto a floured surface; knead in enough remaining flour to make a moderately soft dough that is smooth (3 to 5 minutes total). Shape into a ball. Place in a greased bowl; turn once. Cover; let rise until double (1 to 1¼ hours).

4. Punch down dough. Divide into three portions. Cover; let rest 10 minutes. Meanwhile, grease two large baking sheets; set aside.

5. Shape dough into three round loaves; place on prepared sheets. Cover; let rise until almost double (45 minutes). Preheat oven to 375°F.

6. Beat remaining egg; brush onto loaves. Bake for 35 to 40 minutes or until bread sounds hollow when tapped. If necessary to prevent overbrowning, cover with foil the last 15 to 20 minutes. Remove from baking sheets; cool on a wire rack. Makes 3 loaves (36 servings).

Shortcut Croissants

Prep: 30 minutes Chill: 12 hours
Rise: 2 hours Bake: 20 minutes

- 1 package active dry yeast
- 1 cup lukewarm water (105°F to 115°F)
- 5 cups all-purpose flour
- ¾ cup evaporated milk
- ⅓ cup sugar
- 2 eggs
- ¼ cup butter, melted
- 1½ teaspoons salt
- 1 cup cold butter
- 1 tablespoon water

1. In a medium bowl, dissolve yeast in the 1 cup warm water; let stand for 5 minutes.

2. Add *1 cup* of the flour, the evaporated milk, sugar, *one* of the eggs, melted butter, and salt; beat with an electric mixer on medium speed until smooth. Set aside.

3. In a large bowl, using a pastry blender, cut the cold butter into remaining *4 cups* flour until pieces are pea-size. Add yeast mixture; stir until evenly moistened. Cover; chill in refrigerator for 12 hours to 3 days.

4. Divide dough into four portions. On lightly floured surface, roll one portion to a 14-inch round (keep remaining portions chilled until needed). Cut circle into eight wedges. Starting at the rounded edge, roll each wedge loosely toward the tip. Arrange, tip sides down, 1½ inches apart on an ungreased baking sheet. Repeat with remaining dough. Curve each slightly to form a crescent. Cover; let rise in a warm place until nearly double in size (2 to 2½ hours). Preheat oven to 325°F.

5. In a small bowl, use a fork to beat together remaining egg and the 1 tablespoon water; brush onto crescents. Bake for 20 to 22 minutes or until golden. Remove from baking sheet. Serve warm or cool on a wire rack. Makes 32 croissants.

Rich Cherry Brioches

Prep: 1 hour Chill: 8 hours
Rise: 1 hour Bake: 12 minutes

- 1 package active dry yeast
- ¼ cup lukewarm water (105°F to 115°F)
- ½ cup butter, softened
- ⅓ cup sugar
- 1 teaspoon salt
- 4 cups all-purpose flour
- ½ cup milk
- 4 eggs
- 1¼ cups dried cherries, cranberries, currants, and/or chopped candied citron
- 1 tablespoon sugar

1. In a small bowl, dissolve the yeast in warm water; let stand for 5 minutes.

2. In a large bowl, beat together butter, the ⅓ cup sugar, and the salt with an electric mixer on medium to high speed until fluffy. Add *1 cup* of the flour and the milk. Separate *one* of the eggs. Add the egg yolk and the three whole eggs to the beaten mixture. (Cover and refrigerate remaining egg white.) Add yeast mixture to flour mixture; beat well. Using a wooden spoon, stir in fruit. Stir in the remaining flour.

3. Shape dough into a ball. Place in a lightly greased bowl; turn once to grease surface. Cover; chill dough for 8 to 24 hours.

4. Punch down dough. Turn out dough onto a floured surface. Divide dough into four portions. Cover; let rest for 10 minutes. Meanwhile, grease twenty-four 2½-inch muffin cups; set aside.

5. Divide three dough portions each into eight pieces (24 pieces total). Roll pieces into balls; place in prepared muffin cups. Divide remaining dough portion into 24 pieces; shape into small balls. With thumb, make an indentation in middle of each large ball. Press a small ball into each indentation. In a small bowl, use a fork to stir together reserved egg white and 1 tablespoon sugar; brush onto rolls. Cover; let rise in a warm place until nearly double in size (about 1 hour). Preheat oven to 375°F.

6. Bake for 12 to 14 minutes or until golden. Remove from muffin cups. Cool on a wire rack. Makes 24 rolls.

Christ's Bread
Christopsomo (krihs-TOP-soh-moh)
Prep: 30 minutes **Rise:** 1½ hours
Bake: 45 minutes

- 1   package active dry yeast
- 1   cup lukewarm milk (105°F to 115°F)
- 4   to 4¼ cups all-purpose flour
- 1   tablespoon finely shredded orange peel
- ½   teaspoon salt
- ½   teaspoon ground cardamom
- ¼   to ½ teaspoon anise seeds, crushed
- ¼   teaspoon ground cinnamon
- 2   eggs
- ⅔   cup granulated sugar
- ¼   cup butter, softened
- ½   cup finely chopped almonds
- ½   cup golden raisins
- ¼   cup snipped candied lemon peel (optional)
- 1   egg white
- 1   tablespoon water
- 2   tablespoons coarse sugar

1. In a small bowl, dissolve yeast in warm milk; let stand for 5 minutes.

2. In a large bowl, stir together *4 cups* of the flour, the orange peel, salt, cardamom, anise seeds, and cinnamon; set aside.

3. In a large bowl, combine yeast mixture, eggs, granulated sugar, and butter; beat with an electric mixer on low speed about 2 minutes or until mixed, scraping bowl constantly. Using a wooden spoon, stir in almonds, raisins, and, if desired, candied lemon peel. Stir in flour mixture.

4. Turn out dough onto a lightly floured surface. Knead in enough of the remaining flour to make a moderately soft dough that is smooth and elastic (3 to 5 minutes total). Place in a lightly greased bowl; turn once to grease the surface. Cover and let rise in a warm place until double in size (1 to 1¼ hours).

5. Punch down dough. Turn out onto a lightly floured surface. Cover; let rest for 10 minutes. Grease a 9×1½-inch round baking pan; set aside.

6. Remove ⅔ *cup* of the dough; set remaining dough aside. Divide the ⅔ cup dough into four portions; shape each portion into a 10-inch-long rope. Set aside. Shape the remaining dough into an 8-inch round loaf; place in the prepared baking pan. Twist two ropes together; repeat with remaining ropes. Place twisted ropes on top of the loaf in the shape of a cross. Cover; let rise until nearly double in size (30 to 40 minutes). Preheat oven to 350°F.

7. In a small bowl, use a fork to stir together egg white and the water; brush onto loaf. Sprinkle with coarse sugar. Bake about 45 minutes or until bread sounds hollow when tapped. If necessary to prevent overbrowning, cover with foil the last 10 to 15 minutes of baking. Cool in the pan for 5 minutes. Remove from the pan. Cool on a wire rack. Makes 1 loaf (16 servings).

Make-Ahead Tip: Prepare Christ's Bread as directed. Wrap cooled bread in plastic wrap or foil. Store at room temperature for up to 3 days. (Or place cooled bread in freezer bag; freeze for up to 2 months.)

Christ's Bread

In Greece, Christmas usually begins with the feast of St. Nicholas on December 6, and this round loaf is an important part of the celebration—topped with a braided cross to symbolize Christ. (Cooks have also decorated the bread with symbols representing the family's livelihood, such as fish for fishermen or lambs for sheep farmers.) Serve this licorice-flavored bread for a holiday dinner or as a breakfast loaf.

Cinnamon Fritters
Buñuelos (boo-NWAY-lohz)
Prep: 40 minutes Cook: 2 minutes per batch

- **2** cups all-purpose flour
- **2** tablespoons sugar
- **1** teaspoon baking powder
- **¼** teaspoon salt
- **2** tablespoons shortening
- **2** eggs
- **⅓** cup milk
- **Cooking oil**
- **Sugar or 1 recipe Cinnamon Sugar or Sugar Syrup (right)**

1. In a medium bowl, stir together flour, sugar, baking powder, and salt. Using a pastry blender, cut in shortening until mixture resembles coarse crumbs. Make a well in the center; set aside.

2. In a small bowl, use a fork to beat eggs; stir in milk. Add egg mixture all at once to flour mixture. Stir just until dough clings together.

3. Turn out dough onto a lightly floured surface. Gently knead dough by folding and pressing about 2 minutes or until smooth. Divide dough into 24 portions; shape each portion into a ball. Cover; let rest for 20 minutes.

4. In a heavy 10-inch skillet, heat ¾ inch cooking oil to 375°F. Meanwhile, on a lightly floured surface, roll each ball into a 4-inch round.

5. Fry rounds, two or three at a time, in hot oil for 2 to 3 minutes or until golden, turning once. Drain on paper towels. Keep warm while frying remaining. Top with additional sugar, Cinnamon Sugar, or Sugar Syrup. Makes 24 fritters.

Cinnamon Sugar: In a bowl, stir together ½ cup sugar and 1 teaspoon ground cinnamon.

Sugar Syrup: In a small saucepan, combine ½ cup granulated sugar, ¼ cup packed brown sugar, ¼ cup water, and 1 tablespoon light-colored corn syrup or honey. Bring to boiling; reduce heat. Simmer gently, without stirring, about 20 minutes or until thickened.

Cinnamon Fritters

On December 16 in Mexico, nine days of the ritual known as the posadas begin. Reenacting the pilgrimage of Joseph and Mary seeking shelter for the Christ child's birth, families gather and journey from house to house singing a song to ask for lodging. The first two houses pretend to refuse them, but the third invites them in. Prayers and a celebration follow, often with these crisp fritters—known as *buñuelos*—as part of the holiday festivities.

Soda Bread

Prep: 20 minutes Bake: 35 minutes
Cool: 30 minutes

> 2   cups all-purpose flour
> 1   cup whole wheat flour
> 1   teaspoon baking soda
> 1   teaspoon cream of tartar
> ¼   teaspoon salt
> ¼   cup butter
> 2   eggs
> 1   cup buttermilk or sour milk*
> 2   tablespoons brown sugar
> ½   cup raisins (optional)

1. Grease a baking sheet; set aside. In a medium bowl, stir together all-purpose flour, whole wheat flour, baking soda, cream of tartar, and salt. Using a pastry blender, cut in butter until mixture resembles coarse crumbs. Make a well in the center; set aside.

2. In a small bowl, use a fork to beat one of the eggs; stir in the buttermilk or sour milk and brown sugar. If desired, stir in raisins. Add egg mixture all at once to flour mixture. Stir just until moistened. Preheat oven to 375°F.

3. Turn out dough onto a lightly floured surface. Gently knead dough by folding and pressing for 10 to 12 strokes or until dough is nearly smooth. Shape into a 6-inch round loaf. Place on the prepared baking sheet. Cut a 4×½-inch-long cross in the top. Use a fork to beat remaining egg; brush onto loaf.

4. Bake about 35 minutes or until golden. Remove bread from baking sheet. Cool on a wire rack about 30 minutes. Serve warm. Makes 1 loaf (10 servings).

*Note: To make 1 cup sour milk, place 1 tablespoon lemon juice or vinegar in a glass measuring cup; add enough milk to make 1 cup total liquid. Stir. Let stand for 5 minutes.

Biscuitlike scones were created by the Scots, and legend has it that their name derives from the Stone of Destiny (or Scone), the site where Scottish kings once were crowned. Below is a traditional tearoom version, right down to the currants. For a well-deserved break during the holiday season, enjoy them split and slathered with butter, jam, and whipped or clotted (Devonshire) cream, available at some gourmet markets. Serve them with a brisk cup of tea, of course.

Currant and Cream Scones

Prep: 20 minutes Bake: 12 minutes

> 2   cups all-purpose flour
> ½   cup granulated sugar
> 2½   teaspoons baking powder
> ¼   teaspoon salt
> ½   cup butter
> ½   cup dried currants or coarsely chopped
>   dried tart cherries
> ⅔   cup half-and-half or light cream
> **Coarse sugar**

1. In a large bowl, stir together flour, the ½ cup sugar, the baking powder, and salt. Using a pastry blender, cut in butter until the mixture resembles coarse crumbs. Stir in currants. Make a well in the center. Add ½ cup of the half-and-half, stirring just until flour mixture is moistened. Preheat oven to 350°F.

2. Turn out dough onto a lightly floured surface. Gently knead by folding and pressing for 6 to 8 strokes or just until dough holds together. Divide dough in half. Pat each half to a 6-inch round. Cut each round into eight wedges.

3. Arrange scones 1 inch apart on an ungreased baking sheet. Brush with remaining half-and-half; sprinkle with coarse sugar.

4. Bake for 12 to 15 minutes or until bottoms are golden. Remove scones from baking sheet. Cool on a wire rack for 5 minutes. Serve warm. Makes 16 scones.

New-World Desserts

THE DESSERTS of Christmas carry with them beloved holiday traditions and folklore. Find an almond in your rice pudding in Denmark, and you'll soon be lucky or married or both! In Russia, sweet yeast cakes take the shape of the skirts of the gift-bearing *baba* or grandmother. And what could be more traditional than English cooks stirring up *Mincemeat Tarts* or *Steamed Plum Pudding*—two desserts immortalized in Charles Dickens' *A Christmas Carol?* In this chapter, we've gathered a world of great dessert traditions—each ready to regale your guests with a legendary finish to your holiday meal.

Cherry-Coconut Cake
(recipe, page 88)

87

Mascarpone Cream Tarts
Pictured on page 102.
Prep: 45 minutes Chill: 2 hours
Bake: 10 minutes

  2 17.3-ounce packages (4 sheets) frozen
     puff pastry sheets, thawed
  1 8-ounce carton mascarpone cheese,
     softened (1 cup)
  1 recipe Pastry Cream (below)
Sliced carambola (star fruit) and/or kiwifruit,
     sliced and cut into wedges (optional)

1. Preheat oven to 400°F. For tart shells, unfold pastry sheets on a lightly floured surface. Roll lightly to minimize ridges. Using a 2-inch round cookie cutter, cut out 64 rounds. Place *half* of the rounds on a ungreased baking sheets; prick each a few times with a fork. Using a 1¼-inch round cutter, cut out the middle from the remaining rounds; discard center cutouts.

2. Brush water onto edges of rounds on baking sheet; top with rounds that have the centers cut out. Press gently to seal layers together to form tart shells. Bake for 10 to 12 minutes or until puffed and golden. Remove; cool on wire racks.

3. Up to 1 hour before serving, add the mascarpone cheese to chilled Pastry Cream; beat with an electric mixer on low speed until smooth.

4. Using your fingers, gently press down pastry in centers of tarts to remove air and enlarge centers. (This allows more room for filling.) Carefully spoon mascarpone mixture into tart shells. To serve, arrange fruit pieces on top of the filled tarts. Makes 32 tarts.

Pastry Cream: In a medium saucepan, stir together ⅓ cup sugar and ¼ cup all-purpose flour; stir in 1 cup milk. Add 3 slightly beaten egg yolks; beat until smooth. Cook and stir over medium heat until thickened and bubbly. Remove from heat. Stir in 2 tablespoons liqueur (such as clear crème de cacao, raspberry, or orange) or 1 teaspoon vanilla. Pour into a bowl; cover surface with plastic wrap. Chill for 2 to 4 hours.

Almond Cake Ring
Mandel Kuchen
(MAHN-duhl KOO-khehn)
Stand: 30 minutes Prep: 20 minutes
Bake: 40 minutes Cool: 10 minutes

  4 eggs
  1 tablespoon butter, softened
  2 tablespoons fine dry bread crumbs
3½ cups all-purpose flour
  1 tablespoon baking powder
Dash salt
1¼ cups sugar
  1 cup butter, softened
  1 teaspoon vanilla
  1 teaspoon almond extract
  ½ cup milk
  ½ cup slivered almonds, toasted
  1 recipe Almond Icing (below) (optional)
Slivered almonds, toasted (optional)

1. Let eggs stand at room temperature for 30 minutes. Meanwhile, lightly coat bottom and side of a 10-inch tube pan with the 1 tablespoon softened butter. Sprinkle bread crumbs evenly onto the bottom and two-thirds of the way up the side of the pan; shake out any excess crumbs. In a medium bowl, stir together flour, baking powder, and salt; set aside. Preheat oven to 350°F.

2. In a large bowl, combine sugar and 1 cup butter; beat with an electric mixer on medium to high speed until light and fluffy. Add eggs, *one* at a time, beating well after each addition. Beat in vanilla and almond extract.

3. Alternately add flour mixture and milk to egg mixture, beating on low speed just until combined. Stir in ½ cup almonds. Spoon batter evenly into the prepared pan.

4. Bake for 40 to 45 minutes or until a wooden toothpick inserted in center comes out clean. Cool in pan on a wire rack for 10 minutes. Using a knife or metal spatula, loosen edges from pan. Remove cake from pan; cool on the wire rack. If desired, drizzle with Almond Icing; sprinkle with additional almonds. Makes 12 servings.

Almond Icing: In a small bowl, stir together 1 cup sifted powdered sugar, 1 tablespoon milk, and ¼ teaspoon almond extract. Stir in enough additional milk, 1 teaspoon at a time, to make an icing of drizzling consistency.

Raspberry Meringue Torte

Stand: 1 hour **Prep:** 45 minutes
Bake: 30 minutes **Cool:** 10 minutes **Chill:** 1 hour

- 1 **cup butter**
- 4 **eggs**
- 2 **cups all-purpose flour**
- 1 **teaspoon baking powder**
- ¼ **teaspoon ground allspice (optional)**
- 1 **cup sugar**
- 1 **teaspoon vanilla**
- ½ **cup water**
- ¼ **cup sugar**
- ¼ **cup light rum**
- ¾ **cup seedless raspberry preserves**
- 1 **recipe Soft Meringue (right)**

1. Let butter and eggs stand at room temperature for 30 minutes. Meanwhile, grease and lightly flour two 9×1½-inch round cake pans; set aside. In a small bowl, stir together flour, baking powder, and, if desired, allspice; set aside. Preheat oven to 325°F.

2. In a large bowl, beat butter with an electric mixer on medium to high speed for 30 seconds. Gradually add the 1 cup sugar, *2 tablespoons* at a time, beating on medium speed until mixed and scraping side of bowl. Beat on medium speed for 2 minutes more. Add eggs, *one* at a time, beating after each addition (about 1 minute total). Beat in vanilla. Gradually add flour mixture to butter mixture, beating on low to medium speed just until combined. Spread evenly in prepared pans.

3. Bake for 25 to 30 minutes or until a wooden toothpick inserted near the centers comes out clean. Cool in pans on a wire rack for 10 minutes. Remove from pans; cool on a wire rack.

4. For rum syrup, in a small saucepan, combine the water and the ¼ cup sugar; bring to boiling. Boil, uncovered, for 2 minutes. Remove from heat; stir in rum. Cool.

5. To assemble, place a cake layer on the bottom of a 9-inch springform pan without side. Place on a baking sheet or ovenproof platter. Using a fork, poke holes in the cake layer; spoon *half* of the rum syrup over cake. Spread with the raspberry preserves. Top with second cake layer; spoon the remaining rum syrup over cake.

6. Preheat oven to 450°F. Spread about *half* of the Soft Meringue over cake. Using a pastry bag fitted with a large star tip, pipe the remaining Meringue to decorate cake. Bake about 5 minutes or until light brown. Loosely cover; chill for 1 to 24 hours. Makes 12 to 16 servings.

Soft Meringue: In the large bowl of the freestanding electric mixer, let 4 egg whites stand at room temperature for 30 minutes. Add ¼ teaspoon cream of tartar. Beat with a freestanding electric mixer on medium speed until soft peaks form (tips curl). Gradually add ⅓ cup sugar, beating on high speed until stiff peaks form (tips stand straight). In a small saucepan, combine 1½ cups sugar and ¼ cup water; cook and stir over medium heat until boiling. Clip a candy thermometer to side of saucepan. Cook, without stirring, until the thermometer registers 245° to 250°F. Remove saucepan from heat. Immediately pour the hot sugar mixture in a steady stream into egg white mixture, beating on low speed. Continue beating about 4 minutes or until cool.

Make-Ahead Tip: Prepare the cakes for Raspberry Meringue Torte as directed through step 3. Place each cake layer in a resealable freezer bag; seal. Freeze for up to 3 months. Thaw overnight in the refrigerator. Continue as directed in steps 4, 5, and 6.

Hazelnut Torte

Hazelnut Torte
Haselnuss Torte (HAH-zel-nus TOR-tah)
Also pictured on the cover.
Stand: 30 minutes Prep: 45 minutes
Bake: 15 minutes Cool: 10 minutes

  6 **eggs**
2¼ **cups hazelnuts (filberts)**
  1 **cup sugar**
  ⅓ **cup fine dry bread crumbs**
  3 **tablespoons all-purpose flour**
  1 **teaspoon baking powder**
  ½ **teaspoon ground cinnamon**
  ¼ **teaspoon salt**
  ⅓ **cup seedless red raspberry preserves**
  1 **recipe Mocha Butter Cream Frosting**
      (opposite)
Fresh red raspberries (optional)

1. Separate eggs, placing whites in a large bowl and yolks in another large bowl. Let egg whites and yolks stand at room temperature for 30 minutes. Meanwhile, grease and lightly flour three 9×1½-inch round cake pans; set aside. Preheat oven to 350°F.

2. Spread hazelnuts in a shallow baking pan. Bake about 15 minutes or until toasted. While nuts are warm, rub in a kitchen towel to remove most of the skin. Cool.

3. In a food processor bowl, combine *2 cups* of the hazelnuts and ¼ *cup* of the sugar; cover and process until nuts are finely ground. In a medium bowl, combine nut mixture, bread crumbs, flour, baking powder, and cinnamon; toss until mixed. Set aside. Process remaining ¼ *cup* hazelnuts in a food processor until finely chopped; set aside.

4. Preheat oven to 350°F. Beat egg yolks with an electric mixer on high about 5 minutes or until thickened and lemon-colored. Gradually beat in remaining ¼ *cup* sugar until thick. Set aside.

5. Thoroughly wash beaters. Add salt to egg whites in bowl; beat with an electric mixer on medium speed until soft peaks form (tips curl). Gradually add ½ *cup* of the sugar, beating until stiff peaks form (tips stand straight); set aside.

6. Fold *one-fourth* of the beaten egg whites into yolk mixture. Fold in nut-bread crumb mixture; gently fold into remaining egg whites just until combined. Divide batter among prepared pans. Bake about 15 minutes or until light brown and top springs back when lightly touched. Cool in pans on a wire rack for 10 minutes; remove from pans. Cool on wire rack.

7. To assemble, place a cake layer on a platter; spread with *half* of the preserves. Spread with ¾ *cup* of the Mocha Butter Cream Frosting. Top with a second cake layer; spread with remaining preserves and ¾ *cup* of the frosting. Top with remaining cake layer. Spread side and top of cake with remaining frosting. Using a pastry bag fitted with a large star tip, pipe some of the frosting around top edge. Press finely chopped hazelnuts around lower edge of cake. If desired, top with raspberries. Makes 16 to 20 servings.

Mocha Butter Cream Frosting: In a small bowl, combine 3 tablespoons milk and 1 tablespoon instant coffee crystals; stir until dissolved. In another small bowl, beat ¾ cup softened butter with an electric mixer on medium speed until light and fluffy. Beat in 2 ounces melted and cooled unsweetened chocolate. Gradually add 3 cups sifted powdered sugar, beating until combined. Beat in coffee mixture, 2 tablespoons brandy or orange juice, and 1 teaspoon vanilla. Gradually beat in 1 cup sifted powdered sugar. Beat on high speed for 1 minute or until light and fluffy. Beat in additional milk or powdered sugar, if necessary, to make a frosting of spreading consistency.

Make-Ahead Tip: Prepare Hazelnut Torte as directed. Cover loosely; chill for up to 24 hours.

Raspberry-Apricot Tart
Linzer Torte (LIHN-zuhr TOR-tah)
Prep: 1 hour Chill: 10 hours Bake: 45 minutes
Cool: 1 hour Stand: 2 hours

 1¾ cups all-purpose flour
 1   cup blanched almonds, finely ground
 ½   cup extra-fine granulated sugar
 1   tablespoon finely shredded lemon peel
 ¼   teaspoon salt
 ⅛   teaspoon ground cloves
 ⅛   teaspoon ground cinnamon
 1   cup unsalted butter, softened
 2   egg yolks
 2   teaspoons vanilla
 ¾   cup raspberry preserves
 ¾   cup apricot preserves
 1   egg yolk
 1   tablespoon whipping cream
 Sifted powdered sugar (optional)

1. In a large bowl, stir together flour, almonds, granulated sugar, lemon peel, salt, cloves, and cinnamon. Using a wooden spoon, beat in butter, yolks, and vanilla. Place dough on a large piece of plastic wrap set on a baking sheet; pat into a 10×6-inch rectangle. Wrap and chill for 1½ hours.

2. Combine raspberry and apricot preserves. Cutting dough rectangle crosswise, cut off *three-fourths* of the dough. Shape remaining dough into a ball; cover and chill. Cut dough rectangle crosswise into ⅜-inch-wide strips. Arrange on bottom and around side of a 10-inch springform pan. Press onto bottom and 1 inch up side to form an even crust. Spread preserves mixture onto crust.

3. Place ball of dough on a lightly floured surface. Roll to a 10×6-inch rectangle. Using a floured pastry wheel, cut dough lengthwise into ½-inch-wide strips. Carefully lay *six* strips across top of torte. Give pan a quarter turn and lay remaining strips on top, forming a diamond pattern. Press ends of strips into rim of bottom crust, trimming ends as necessary. Crimp top edge of crust with a fork. Beat egg yolk; stir in cream. Brush yolk mixture onto strips and edges. Chill for 20 minutes. Preheat oven to 350°F.

4. Bake for 45 to 50 minutes or until golden. Cool in pan on a wire rack for 1 hour; loosen side of pan. Cover; chill for 8 to 24 hours. Let stand at room temperature for 2 hours. If desired, sprinkle with powdered sugar. Makes 16 servings.

Burnt Cream
Crème Brûlée (krehm broo-LAY)
Prep: 10 minutes Bake: 35 minutes
Chill: 1 hour Stand: 20 minutes

- 2 **cups half-and-half or light cream**
- 5 **egg yolks**
- ⅓ **cup sugar**
- 1 **teaspoon vanilla**
- ⅛ **teaspoon salt**
- ¼ **cup sugar**

1. Preheat oven to 325°F. In a heavy, small saucepan, heat half-and-half over medium-low heat just until bubbly, stirring occasionally. Remove from heat; set aside.

2. Meanwhile, in a medium bowl, beat egg yolks slightly; beat in the ⅓ cup sugar, the vanilla, and salt. Slowly beat in hot half-and-half.

3. Place six 6-ounce soufflé dishes or custard cups in a 3-quart rectangular baking dish. Place baking dish on oven rack. Divide yolk mixture evenly among cups. Pour enough boiling water into dish to reach halfway up sides of cups.

4. Bake for 35 to 40 minutes or until a knife inserted near the center of each custard comes out clean. Remove cups from the water; cool on a wire rack. Cover and chill for 1 to 8 hours.

5. Before serving, let custards stand at room temperature for 20 minutes. Meanwhile, to caramelize sugar, in a heavy, 8-inch skillet, heat the ¼ cup sugar over medium-high heat until sugar begins to melt, shaking skillet occasionally to heat sugar evenly. *Do not stir.* Once the sugar starts to melt, reduce heat to low. Cook about 5 minutes more or until all of the sugar is melted and golden, stirring as needed with a wooden spoon. Quickly drizzle the caramelized sugar over custards. (If sugar starts to harden in the skillet, return to heat, stirring until melted.) Serve immediately. If desired, garnish with an edible flower. Makes 6 servings.

Amaretto Burnt Cream: Prepare Burnt Cream as directed, except decrease half-and-half or light cream to 1¾ cups and stir 2 tablespoons amaretto, crème de cacao, or coffee liqueur into the egg yolk mixture.

Burnt Cream

Trifle often makes its way to the English holiday table, especially when a light-textured dessert is desired after a heavy meal. Trifles—affectionately known as "tipsy cakes" because of their hallmark touch of spirits—are particularly good choices when you're serving an array of desserts because guests can easily help themselves to a spoonful; plus, trifles provide an airy contrast to dense cakes and pies on the buffet.

Orange Marmalade Trifles

Orange Marmalade Trifles
Prep: 30 minutes Chill: 3 hours

3	eggs
¼	cup granulated sugar
2	cups milk
½	teaspoon vanilla
1	10¾-ounce frozen pound cake
1	10-ounce jar orange marmalade
½	cup chopped hazelnuts (filberts) or walnuts
2	to 3 tablespoons orange liqueur, hazelnut liqueur, sherry, or apricot nectar
1	cup whipping cream
2	tablespoons sifted powdered sugar

1. For custard sauce, in a medium saucepan, use a rotary beater or whisk to beat eggs and granulated sugar just until combined. Stir in milk. Cook and stir over medium heat just until mixture coats the back of a clean metal spoon.

Remove from heat. Stir in vanilla. Place saucepan in ice water to quickly cool mixture. Pour cooled custard sauce into a bowl; cover surface with plastic wrap. Chill for 1 hour.

2. Cut pound cake into 1-inch cubes; set aside. In a small saucepan, heat marmalade just until melted; set aside.

3. Divide *half* of the cake cubes among eight parfait glasses or arrange in the bottom of a 2-quart glass serving bowl. Drizzle with *half* of the melted orange marmalade. Sprinkle with *half* of the hazelnuts or walnuts. Sprinkle with *half* of the liqueur, rum, or apricot nectar. Spoon *half* of the custard sauce over all. Repeat layering with remaining cake cubes, marmalade, nuts, liqueur, and custard sauce. Cover; chill for 2 to 6 hours. Chill a medium bowl and beaters of mixer.

4. Before serving, in the chilled bowl, combine whipping cream and powdered sugar; beat with the chilled beaters with electric mixer on medium speed until soft peaks form (tips curl). Spoon cream onto desserts. Makes 8 servings.

Mincemeat Tart

British cooks stir up their mincemeat on stir-up Sunday at the end of November, when they make *Steamed Plum Pudding*. Freshly baked *Mincemeat Tarts* appear throughout the Christmas season, often after Midnight Mass and on New Year's Eve, when it's customary to make a wish with the first bite of mincemeat.

Mincemeat Tart
Prep: 1 hour Bake: 20 minutes

- 1 **medium orange**
- 3 **medium tart cooking apples (such as Granny Smith), peeled, cored, and coarsely chopped**
- ⅔ **cup granulated sugar**
- ½ **cup golden raisins**
- ½ **cup dried cranberries or dried currants**
- ½ **cup dates or pitted dried plums (prunes), snipped**
- ½ **cup diced mixed candied fruits and peels or snipped dried apple**
- ½ **cup apple juice, apple cider, or orange juice**
- ¼ **cup brandy**
- 1 **teaspoon finely shredded lemon peel**
- 2 **tablespoons lemon juice**
- 2 **teaspoons apple pie spice**
- ¾ **cup chopped walnuts or almonds**
- 1 **recipe Tart Pastry (right)**
- 2 **tablespoons butter**

Milk

Coarse sugar

Sugared lemon peel and/or orange peel*
(optional)

1. For filling, cut up the orange, removing any seeds; place unpeeled orange pieces in a food processor bowl. Cover; process until chopped.

2. In a large saucepan, combine chopped unpeeled orange, coarsely chopped apples, the ⅔ cup granulated sugar, the raisins, cranberries or currants, dates or dried plums, candied fruits and peels or dried apple, apple juice, brandy, the 1 teaspoon lemon peel, the lemon juice, and apple pie spice. Bring to boiling; reduce heat. Simmer, uncovered, for 10 to 15 minutes or until slightly thickened, stirring occasionally. Remove from heat; cool. Stir in nuts; set aside.

3. Preheat oven to 425°F. Grease a very large baking sheet; set aside. On a lightly floured surface, roll Tart Pastry to an 18×12-inch oval. Wrap pastry around rolling pin. Transfer to the prepared baking sheet.

4. Spoon filling into the center of the pastry oval, spreading to within 2 inches of the edges. Dot filling with butter. Fold edges of pastry up and over the filling, leaving filling in center exposed and pleating pastry as necessary. Brush folded edges of tart with milk; sprinkle with coarse sugar.

5. Bake for 20 to 25 minutes or until pastry is golden and filling is bubbly. Cool on the baking sheet on a wire rack. If desired, garnish with sugared peel. Makes 16 servings.

Tart Pastry: In a large bowl, combine 2 cups all-purpose flour and ½ teaspoon salt. Using a pastry blender, cut in ⅔ cup shortening until pieces are pea-size. Sprinkle 1 tablespoon cold water over part of the mixture; gently toss with a fork. Push moistened dough to side of bowl. Repeat, using 1 tablespoon cold water at a time (6 to 7 tablespoons cold water total), until all of the flour mixture is moistened. Shape into a ball.

Make-Ahead Tip: Prepare Mincemeat Tart as directed through step 2, except do not stir in nuts. Cover and store in the refrigerator for up to 2 days. Stir in the nuts. Continue as directed in steps 3, 4, and 5.

*Note: For sugared citrus peel, dip coarsely shredded lemon peel and/or orange peel into light-colored corn syrup; dip the peel into granulated sugar, gently tossing to coat.

Stout Fruitcake

Prep: 20 minutes Bake: 70 minutes
Cool: 15 minutes

3¾ cups all-purpose flour
2 teaspoons baking powder
½ teaspoon baking soda
1½ cups butter, softened
1½ cups packed brown sugar
4 eggs
1½ cups stout beer (12 ounces)
1 cup raisins or dried currants
1 cup diced mixed candied fruits and
  peels
Sifted powdered sugar (optional)

1. Preheat oven to 325°F. Grease and lightly flour a 10-inch fluted tube pan; set aside. In a medium bowl, stir together flour, baking powder, and baking soda; set aside.

2. In a large bowl, combine butter and brown sugar; beat with an electric mixer on medium to high speed until light and fluffy. Add eggs, *one at a time*, beating well after each addition. Alternately add flour mixture and stout to egg mixture, beating on low speed just until combined. Fold in raisins or currants and candied fruits and peels. Spoon batter into prepared pan.

3. Bake about 70 minutes or until top springs back when lightly touched and a wooden toothpick inserted near the center comes out clean. Cool in pan on a wire rack for 15 minutes. Remove from pan; cool on the wire rack. If desired, sprinkle with powdered sugar. Makes 20 servings.

Steamed Plum Pudding

Stand: 2 hours Prep: 40 minutes
Cook: 2¼ hours Cool: 20 minutes

1 cup golden raisins
1 cup dried currants
1 teaspoon *each* finely shredded orange
  peel and lemon peel (set aside)
¼ cup orange juice
2 tablespoons lemon juice
2 tablespoons brandy or orange juice
1 medium apple, peeled and shredded
½ cup chopped almonds
½ cup diced mixed candied fruits and peels

3 cups soft bread crumbs (about 4 slices)
1 cup all-purpose flour
1 teaspoon ground cinnamon
½ teaspoon baking powder
½ teaspoon baking soda
½ teaspoon ground ginger
½ teaspoon ground mace or nutmeg
¼ teaspoon salt
½ cup beef suet or shortening
1 cup packed brown sugar
¼ cup molasses
3 eggs
½ cup milk
1 teaspoon vanilla
1 recipe Hard Sauce (below)

1. In a medium bowl, soak raisins and currants in orange juice, lemon juice, and brandy, covered, in a cool, dry place for 2 hours or overnight. *Do not drain.* Stir in orange peel, lemon peel, apple, almonds, and candied fruits and peels.

2. In a small bowl, stir together crumbs, flour, cinnamon, baking powder, soda, ginger, mace, and salt; set aside.

3. In a large bowl, beat shortening with an electric mixer for 30 seconds. Add brown sugar and molasses; beat until combined. Add eggs, *one at a time*, beating on low speed just until combined (do not overbeat).

4. Alternately add crumb mixture and milk to egg mixture, beating on low speed just until combined. Stir in fruit mixture and vanilla.

5. Grease and flour a 12-cup mold; spread batter in mold. Lightly grease a square of foil; cover mold with foil, pressing tightly against rim. Place on a rack in a deep kettle containing 1 inch of simmering water. Cover; steam about 2¼ hours or until a long wooden skewer inserted near center comes out clean, adding boiling water if necessary. Remove mold; cool on a wire rack for 20 minutes. Carefully invert pudding onto wire rack; remove mold. Cool slightly. Serve with Hard Sauce. Makes 16 servings.

Hard Sauce: In a medium bowl, combine 1¼ cups sifted powdered sugar and ¾ cup softened butter; beat with an electric mixer on medium speed until fluffy. Beat in 3 tablespoons brandy or orange juice and ½ teaspoon vanilla. Cover; chill for up to 2 weeks. Let stand at room temperature for 30 minutes before serving. Makes 1¼ cups.

Lemon Curd Tassies

Prep: 45 minutes Bake: 8 minutes
Cool: 10 minutes Chill: 1 hour

- 1¼ cups all-purpose flour
- ⅓ cup sugar
- 2 teaspoons finely shredded lemon peel
- ½ cup cold butter
- 1 egg yolk
- 2 tablespoons cold water
- 1 recipe Lemon Curd (right)

Lemon peel strips (optional)

1. In a medium bowl, stir together flour, sugar, and shredded lemon peel. Using a pastry blender, cut in cold butter until mixture is crumbly. In a small bowl, beat egg yolk; stir in cold water. Gradually stir egg yolk mixture into flour mixture. Gently knead dough just until a ball forms. If necessary, cover with plastic wrap; chill for 30 to 60 minutes or until easy to handle.

2. Preheat oven to 375°F. For shells, divide dough into 36 pieces. Press each dough piece onto the bottom and up the side of a 1¾-inch muffin cup. Bake for 8 to 10 minutes or until golden.

3. Cool tassie shells in muffin cups on a wire rack for 10 minutes. Remove shells from muffin cups. Spoon *1 rounded teaspoon* of Lemon Curd into each tassie shell; cover with plastic wrap. Chill for 1 to 2 hours before serving. If desired, garnish with lemon peel strips. Makes 36 tassies.

Lemon Curd: In a medium saucepan, stir together ⅔ cup sugar and 1 tablespoon cornstarch. Stir in 2 teaspoons finely shredded lemon peel, ½ cup lemon juice, ¼ cup water, and 2 tablespoons butter. Cook and stir over medium heat until thickened and bubbly. Slowly stir about half of the hot lemon mixture into 3 slightly beaten egg yolks. Return all of the egg yolk mixture to the saucepan, stirring to combine. Bring to boiling; reduce heat. Cook and stir for 2 minutes more. Transfer to a small bowl. Cover surface with plastic wrap; chill for 25 minutes.

Make-Ahead Tip: Prepare Lemon Curd Tassies as directed through step 1. Wrap dough in plastic wrap; freeze up to 1 month. Thaw dough in the refrigerator for 24 hours. Continue as directed in steps 2 and 3.

Maids-of-Honor Tarts, Lemon Curd Tassies, and Mascarpone Cream Tarts (recipe, page 90)

It's hard to find two sources that agree on the origin of the name of Maids-of-Honor Tarts. By most accounts, they've been linked to Henry VIII, who was said to have named them after Anne Boleyn, the maid of honor to the King's sister, Mary, and later the King's wife. While the true story of the tarts may be lost to history, the pleasure of eating these nutty, buttery gems is not!

Maids-of-Honor Tarts
Prep: 45 minutes Bake: 15 minutes

 1   recipe Tiny Tart Pastry (below)
 ⅓   cup sugar
 1   tablespoon butter, softened
 2   teaspoons all-purpose flour
 ⅛   teaspoon ground nutmeg
 1   egg
 1   tablespoon cream sherry
 ½   cup ground almonds
 2   tablespoons red currant jelly or
     strawberry or raspberry jam
Red currant jelly or strawberry or raspberry
     jam, melted (optional)

1. Preheat oven to 375°F. On a lightly floured surface, use your hands to slightly flatten Tiny Tart Pastry. Roll dough to ⅛-inch thickness. Using a 2½-inch round cookie cutter, cut 24 circles from dough, rerolling if necessary. Press each circle onto the bottom and up the side of an ungreased 1¾-inch muffin cup; set aside.

2. For filling, in a medium bowl, beat sugar, butter, flour, and nutmeg with an electric mixer on medium speed until mixed. Beat in eggs and cream sherry; stir in almonds.

3. Spoon a scant ¼ *teaspoon* of the jelly or jam into each dough-lined muffin cup. Top each with about *1 teaspoon* of the filling. Bake for 15 to 20 minutes or until tops are light brown. Remove tarts from muffin cups; cool on a wire rack. If desired, drizzle each tart with some of the melted jelly or jam. Makes 24 tarts.

Tiny Tart Pastry: In a medium bowl, stir together 1¼ cups all-purpose flour, 4 teaspoons sugar, and ¼ teaspoon salt. Using a pastry blender, cut in ⅓ cup cold butter until pieces are pea-size. Sprinkle 1 tablespoon milk over part of the flour mixture; gently toss with a fork. Push moistened dough to the side of the bowl. Repeat moistening the flour mixture, using 3 to 4 tablespoons more milk, 1 tablespoon at a time, until all is moistened. Form dough into a ball.

Plum Torte
Vinarterta (vee-nah-TAR-tah)
Prep: 1¼ hours Bake: 12 minutes per batch
Chill: 24 hours Stand: 2 hours

 2   pounds pitted dried plums (prunes)
 2¼   cups sugar
 4½   cups all-purpose flour
 2   teaspoons baking powder
 ¼   teaspoon ground cardamom
 1   cup butter, softened
 2   eggs
 2   teaspoons vanilla
 ¼   cup half-and-half or light cream
 1   recipe Vanilla Glaze (below)

1. For filling, in a large saucepan, combine dried plums and 3 cups *water*. Bring to boiling; reduce heat. Cover; simmer about 20 minutes or until plums are very soft. Drain, reserving ½ *cup* of the cooking liquid. Cool slightly.

2. In a food processor, combine *half* of the plums and ¼ *cup* of the reserved cooking liquid. Cover; process until smooth; return to saucepan. Repeat. Stir in ¾ *cup* of the sugar. Cook and stir over low heat about 5 minutes or until thick. Cool.

3. Preheat oven to 350°F. Grease two 9×1½-inch round cake pans; line with waxed paper. In a small bowl, stir together flour, baking powder, cardamom, and ½ teaspoon *salt*. Set aside.

4. In a large bowl, beat butter with an electric mixer for 30 seconds. Gradually beat in 1½ *cups* sugar. Add eggs, *one* at a time, beating well after each addition. Beat in vanilla. Alternately add flour mixture and half-and-half, beating until combined. Divide into seven ⅔-cup portions.

5. Pat a portion into a thin layer that covers the bottom of one prepared pan. Repeat with another portion of dough in second pan. Bake for 12 to 15 minutes or until edges are light brown. Invert onto a wire rack; remove waxed paper. Cool on the rack. Repeat until all dough is baked.

6. Place a layer on a serving platter; spread with ⅔ *cup* of the filling. Repeat with remaining layers and filling, ending with plain layer. Spread Vanilla Glaze on top. Cover and chill for 24 hours. Let stand at room temperature for 2 hours before serving. Makes 24 servings.

Vanilla Glaze: Mix 2 cups sifted powdered sugar and 1 teaspoon vanilla. Stir in enough milk (2 to 3 tablespoons) to make drizzling consistency.

Fruit-Filled Pastries

Fruit-Filled Pastries
Kifli (KEE-flee)
Prep: 45 minutes Chill: 8 hours
Bake: 15 minutes

  1   **recipe Sour Cream Pastry (right)**
  ⅔   **cup apricot or apple spreadable fruit**
  ½   **cup finely chopped pecans**
  1   **egg yolk**
  1   **teaspoon water**
     Coarse sugar (optional)

1. Preheat oven to 350°F. On a lightly floured surface, roll each Sour Cream Pastry portion into a 15×10-inch rectangle. Cut into 2½-inch squares (48 total).

2. For filling, in a small bowl, stir together spreadable fruit and pecans. Place a slightly rounded ½ *teaspoon* filling in the center of each square. Fold each square in half diagonally to form a triangle. Seal with a fork.

3. Arrange pastries on an ungreased baking sheet. In a small bowl, beat egg yolk with water; brush onto pastries. If desired, sprinkle with sugar.

4. Bake about 15 minutes or until golden. Transfer to a wire rack. Serve warm, or cool to room temperature. Makes 48 pastries.

Sour Cream Pastry: In a small bowl, dissolve 1 package active dry yeast and 1½ teaspoons granulated sugar in ¼ cup lukewarm milk (105°F to 115°F). In a large bowl, using a pastry blender, cut 1 cup butter into 2 cups all-purpose flour until the mixture is pea-size. Stir in yeast mixture, ½ cup dairy sour cream, and 2 egg yolks. With floured hands, knead until combined. Divide mixture in half; shape into balls. On a floured surface, roll each half of the Sour Cream Pastry into a 12-inch square. Fold each square in thirds; wrap in plastic wrap. Chill for 8 to 24 hours.

Make-Ahead Tip: Prepare and bake Fruit-Filled Pastries as directed. Cool completely. Place pastries in a single layer in freezer containers; freeze for up to 1 month. To serve, arrange frozen pastries on an ungreased baking sheet. Bake in a 350°F oven about 10 minutes or until warm. Serve warm, or cool to room temperature.

Rum Raisin Cakes
Rumovaya Babas
(RUM-ah-vah-yah BAH-bahs)

Prep: 1 hour Rise: 80 minutes
Bake: 15 minutes

2	cups all-purpose flour
1	package active dry yeast
⅓	cup milk
1	tablespoon sugar
½	teaspoon salt
4	eggs
½	cup butter
½	cup raisins
1	teaspoon finely shredded orange peel
1½	cups water
¾	cup sugar
⅓	cup rum
1	recipe Apricot Glaze (right)
1	recipe Cream Sauce (right) (optional)

1. In a large bowl, stir together 1½ *cups* of the flour and the yeast; set aside. In a small saucepan, heat and stir milk, the 1 tablespoon sugar, and the salt just until warm (120°F to 130°F).

2. Add milk mixture to flour mixture. Add eggs. Beat with an electric mixer on low to medium speed for 30 seconds, scraping the side of the bowl constantly. Beat on high speed for 3 minutes. Using a wooden spoon, stir in the remaining flour. (The batter will be soft and sticky.) Cut butter into small pieces; place on top of batter. Cover; let rise in a warm place until double in size (about 1 hour).

3. Grease twelve ½-cup baba molds, twelve 2½-inch muffin cups, or eight popover pan cups; set aside.

4. Stir butter, raisins, and orange peel into the batter. Divide the batter among prepared molds or cups, filling each ½ to ⅔ full. Cover and let rise in a warm place until batter fills molds or cups (20 to 30 minutes). (Or cover and chill for 8 to 24 hours. Let stand at room temperature for 20 minutes.) Preheat oven to 350°F.

5. Bake for 15 to 20 minutes or until golden. Meanwhile, place a wire rack over waxed paper. Remove cakes from molds or cups; cool on the wire rack.

6. For rum syrup, in a heavy, small saucepan, stir together the water and the ¾ cup sugar. Cook and stir over medium heat until the sugar is dissolved. Bring to boiling. Boil, uncovered, without stirring, for 5 minutes. Remove from heat; cool slightly. Stir in the rum.

7. Using a large fork, prick each cake all over. Dip cakes, top sides down, into the rum syrup two or three times or until moistened. Return to wire racks. Spoon any remaining rum syrup over cakes. Brush Apricot Glaze onto cakes.

8. To serve, if desired, spoon Cream Sauce onto eight to twelve dessert plates. Place a cake on each plate. Makes 8 to 12 servings.

Apricot Glaze: If necessary, snip large pieces of apricot in ½ cup apricot preserves. In a small saucepan, combine preserves and 1 tablespoon water. Heat and stir over low heat until melted.

Cream Sauce: In a small bowl, combine ⅓ cup whipping cream and ⅓ cup dairy sour cream.

Rum Raisin Cake

In the heart of Russia, Christmas is generally celebrated on January 6 and 7 (according to the Julian calendar), and it's the kind-hearted Babushka—or Grandmother—who fills the Christmas stockings for children. According to one story, Babushka meant to travel with the Three Wise Men to bear gifts to Jesus, but she was late and couldn't find him. Hence, she continues to wander, leaving presents for good boys and girls. Coincidentally, this legendary rum-soaked cake is called a "baba," another name for grandmother. Cooked in the traditional mold, a baba is thought to resemble a grandmother's skirts.

Apples and Cream Dessert
Aeblekage (ay-bul-KAY)
Prep: 30 minutes Chill: 4 hours

6 medium cooking apples (such as Granny Smith or Rome Beauty), peeled and cut into bite-size pieces (6 cups)
½ cup water
¼ cup sugar
3 inches stick cinnamon
1 cup whipping cream
1½ cups coarsely crumbled amaretti cookies or almond macaroons
½ cup fine dry bread crumbs
½ cup butter, melted
⅛ teaspoon ground nutmeg
½ cup red currant jelly or strawberry preserves
Fresh mint sprigs (optional)

1. In a medium saucepan, combine apples, the water, sugar, and stick cinnamon. Bring to boiling; reduce heat. Cover and simmer for 8 to 10 minutes or until apples are tender. Remove stick cinnamon. Cool apple mixture to room temperature; set aside.

2. Meanwhile, chill a medium bowl and the beaters of an electric mixer. In the chilled bowl, beat the whipping cream with an electric mixer on medium speed until soft peaks form (tips curl); set aside.

3. In another medium bowl, stir together crumbled cookies, bread crumbs, melted butter, and nutmeg. If desired, set aside *1 tablespoon* of the mixture.

4. In a 2-quart straight-sided glass bowl, layer *half* the crumb mixture, *half* the apple mixture, *half* the jelly, and *half* the whipped cream. Repeat layers. Cover and chill for 4 to 8 hours. If desired, just before serving, garnish with reserved crumb mixture and mint. Makes 6 servings.

Cardamom Rice Pudding
Risengrod (REE-sen-grul)
Prep: 30 minutes Bake: 1¼ hours

1½ cups water
½ teaspoon salt
¾ cup short or medium grain rice
2 eggs, slightly beaten
2 cups whipping cream, half-and-half, or light cream
1½ cups milk
⅔ cup sugar
1 tablespoon butter
½ teaspoon ground cardamom
1 blanched whole almond
1 recipe Raspberry Sauce (below)
Fresh red raspberries (optional)

1. In a medium saucepan, combine the water and salt; bring to boiling. Add uncooked rice. Return to boiling; reduce heat. Cover and simmer for 12 to 15 minutes or until the water is absorbed (rice will still be slightly crunchy).

2. Preheat oven to 325°F. Butter a 2-quart casserole. In a large bowl, stir together rice, eggs, cream, milk, sugar, butter, and cardamom.

3. Set the casserole in a large roasting pan on an oven rack. Spoon rice mixture into the prepared casserole. Hide the almond in the rice mixture. Pour boiling water into the roasting pan around the casserole to reach halfway up the side.

4. Bake, uncovered, for 1 hour. Stir mixture. Bake for 15 minutes more. Remove casserole from pan of water. Stir mixture again. (Pudding should have a creamy texture.) Cool slightly.

5. Serve pudding warm with Raspberry Sauce. If desired, garnish with fresh raspberries. Makes 8 to 10 servings.

Raspberry Sauce: Place 1½ cups fresh or thawed red raspberries in a blender container or food processor bowl. Cover; blend or process until berries are smooth. Press berries through a fine-mesh sieve; discard seeds. Repeat with another 1½ cups raspberries. (You should have 1 cup sieved berries.) In a medium saucepan, stir together ⅓ cup sugar and 1 teaspoon cornstarch. Add sieved berries. Cook and stir over medium heat until thickened and bubbly. Cook and stir 2 minutes more. Remove from heat. Cool slightly.

Cardamom Rice Pudding with Raspberry Sauce

When the Danes look forward to rice pudding after their Christmas Eve meal, they're hoping to find a single almond hidden by the cook. The lucky diner who discovers the almond receives a present, often a marzipan pig (recipe, page 137) or other marzipan candy. And if a single woman finds it, lore has it that she won't stay unmarried for long! Your family and friends will love hunting for the almond as much they love eating this sweet, comforting dessert.

107

Honey-Walnut Phyllo Pastries
Baklava (BAHK-lah-vah)
Prep: 45 minutes   Bake: 35 minutes

- **1** pound walnuts, finely chopped (about 4 cups)
- **2** cups sugar
- **1** teaspoon ground cinnamon
- **1¼** cups butter, melted
- **1** 16-ounce package (forty 14x9-inch sheets) frozen phyllo dough, thawed
- **1** cup water
- **¼** cup honey
- **½** teaspoon finely shredded lemon peel
- **2** tablespoons lemon juice
- **2** inches stick cinnamon

1. For filling, in a large bowl, stir together walnuts, ½ *cup* of the sugar, and the ground cinnamon; set aside. Preheat oven to 325°F.

2. Brush the bottom of a 15×10×1-inch baking pan with some of the melted butter. Unfold phyllo dough. (Keep phyllo covered with plastic wrap, removing sheets as you need them.) Layer *ten* of the phyllo sheets in the baking pan, overlapping sheets, generously brushing each sheet with melted butter, and allowing phyllo to extend up sides of pan. Sprinkle about 1⅓ *cups* of the filling onto the phyllo. Repeat layering the phyllo sheets and filling twice.

3. Layer remaining phyllo sheets on the third layer of filling, brushing each sheet with butter before adding the next phyllo sheet. Drizzle any remaining butter over the top layers. Trim edges of phyllo to fit the pan.

4. Using a sharp knife, cut through all the layers to make 60 square-, diamond-, or triangle-shaped pieces. Bake for 35 to 45 minutes or until golden. Cool slightly in pan on a wire rack.

5. Meanwhile, for syrup, in a medium saucepan, stir together the remaining sugar, the water, honey, lemon peel, lemon juice, and stick cinnamon. Bring to boiling; reduce heat. Simmer, uncovered, for 20 minutes. Remove cinnamon. Pour honey mixture over slightly cooled baklava in the pan. Makes about 60 servings.

Honey-Walnut Phyllo Pastries

On Christmas Eve in Greece, children walk from home to home singing carols while beating small clay drums and tinkling metal triangles. Often, they're rewarded with such sweet treats as pastries, cookies, fruits, walnuts, and almonds. Why not reward the young carolers in your family with some nut-studded *Baklava*, a famous Greek pastry? If you wish, try making it with a combination of pistachios, pecans, and walnuts instead of just the walnuts.

Orange Phyllo Diamonds
Galatoboureko (GAH-laht-oh-bur-eck-oh)
Prep: 45 minutes Cool: 1 hour
Bake: 40 minutes Chill: 2 hours

- 2   cups milk
- ¼   cup quick-cooking wheat cereal (farina)
- ⅓   cup sugar
- 1   teaspoon finely shredded orange peel
- 3   tablespoons orange juice
- ½   teaspoon vanilla
- 4   eggs
- ⅓   cup sugar
- ½   of a 16-ounce package frozen phyllo dough (twenty 14x9-inch sheets), thawed
- ½   cup butter, melted
- 1   recipe Spiced Orange Syrup (right)

1. In a medium saucepan, bring milk to a gentle boil. Stir in cereal. Cook and stir about 1 minute or until slightly thickened and smooth. Add ⅓ cup sugar; stir until sugar is dissolved. Remove from heat.

2. Using a whisk, beat in orange peel, orange juice, and vanilla. (The mixture may appear curdled at first, but will become thicker and smooth as you beat it.) Transfer the mixture to a large bowl. Cover surface with plastic wrap; cool for 30 minutes.

3. In a medium bowl, combine eggs and ⅓ cup sugar; beat with an electric mixer on high speed about 4 minutes or until thick and lemon-colored. Fold into farina mixture; set aside.

4. Preheat oven to 350°F. Grease a 13×9×2-inch baking pan; set aside. Place a sheet of phyllo dough in the bottom of the prepared baking pan. Brush with some of the melted butter. Repeat with *nine* more phyllo sheets and melted butter.

5. Pour egg mixture over phyllo layers in baking pan. Cover with remaining phyllo, brushing melted butter between sheets. Bake about 40 minutes or until pastry is golden and filling appears set. Cool in pan on a wire rack.

6. Gradually pour Spiced Orange Syrup over warm baked phyllo. Cool on the wire rack. Cover and chill for 2 to 24 hours. Cut into diamonds to serve. Makes 24 servings.

Spiced Orange Syrup: In a small saucepan, combine ½ cup water, ⅓ cup honey, ¼ cup sugar, 4 inches stick cinnamon, 3 whole cloves, and 1 teaspoon finely shredded orange peel. Bring to boiling; reduce heat. Cover and simmer for 30 minutes. Remove from heat. Stir in 3 tablespoons orange juice and ½ teaspoon vanilla. Cool for 30 minutes. Remove cinnamon and cloves.

Pumpkin Turnovers
Pumpkin Empanadas
(EM-pah-NAH-dahs)
Prep: 45 minutes Chill: 1 hour
Cook: 3 minutes per batch Cool: 15 minutes

- 3   cups all-purpose flour
- 2   teaspoons baking powder
- ½   teaspoon salt
- ½   cup lard or shortening
- 2   eggs
- ½   cup milk
- 1   recipe Pumpkin Filling (below)
- Cooking oil or shortening for deep frying
- Sifted powdered sugar

1. In a medium bowl, stir together flour, baking powder, and salt. Using a pastry blender, cut in the ½ cup lard or shortening until mixture resembles fine crumbs. In a small bowl, beat eggs; stir in milk. Add egg mixture to flour mixture; stir until all is moistened (use hands, if necessary). Form into a ball. Cover and chill for 1 hour.

2. Divide dough into 16 portions. On a lightly floured surface, roll each portion into a 6-inch circle. Place about 3 *tablespoons* of the Pumpkin Filling in the center of each dough circle. Brush edges with water. Fold each circle in half; press edges with a fork to seal.

3. In a heavy saucepan or deep-fat fryer, heat 3 *inches* of cooking oil or melted shortening to 375°F. Fry turnovers, *one* or *two* at a time, in hot fat about 3 minutes or until golden, turning once. Drain on paper towels. Cool for 15 minutes; sprinkle turnovers with powdered sugar. Serve warm. Makes 16 servings.

Pumpkin Filling: Combine one 15-ounce can pumpkin, 1 cup packed brown sugar, ¾ cup chopped walnuts, ½ cup raisins, 1 teaspoon ground cinnamon, and ¼ teaspoon ground cloves.

Raisin Bread Pudding
Capirotada (kay-pir-oh-TAH-dah)
Prep: 30 minutes Bake: 25 minutes

    2 cups sugar
    2½ cups water
    ¼ cup butter
    1½ teaspoons ground cinnamon
    1 teaspoon vanilla
    1 16-ounce loaf white bread, cut into
       cubes and toasted (about 16 cups)
    4 ounces cheddar cheese, shredded
       (1 cup)
    1 cup raisins
    Whipped cream (optional)

1. Preheat oven to 350°F. To caramelize sugar, in a heavy, 3-quart saucepan, heat the sugar over medium-high heat until sugar begins to melt, shaking skillet occasionally to heat sugar evenly. *Do not stir.* Once the sugar starts to melt, reduce heat to low. Cook about 5 minutes more or until all of the sugar is melted and golden, stirring as needed with a wooden spoon. Remove from heat. Carefully add the water (it will splatter). Return saucepan to heat. Bring to boiling, stirring to melt hardened sugar lumps. Remove from heat. Stir in butter, cinnamon, and vanilla.

2. In a 3-quart rectangular baking dish, arrange *half* of the bread cubes. Sprinkle *half* of the cheese and all of the raisins over bread cubes. Top with the remaining bread cubes and cheese. Pour caramelized sugar mixture over all.

3. Bake, uncovered, for 25 to 30 minutes or until top is golden and syrup is absorbed. Serve warm. If desired, serve with whipped cream. Makes 16 servings.

In Mexico, cooks bake *Capirotada* at Eastertime, however, in New Mexico, it's often served on Christmas Eve. There are many recipes for this treasured bread pudding; most, however, include eggs, cheese, and aromatic spices, such as cinnamon or cloves.

Flan
Prep: 30 minutes Stand: 10 minutes
Bake: 35 minutes Cool: 1 hour Chill: 2 hours

    ⅔ cup sugar
    3 eggs
    2 egg yolks
    2 cups whole milk
    1 14-ounce can (1⅓ cups) sweetened
       condensed milk
    1 tablespoon vanilla

1. Preheat oven to 350°F. To caramelize sugar, in a heavy, large skillet, heat sugar over medium-high heat until sugar begins to melt, shaking skillet occasionally to heat sugar evenly. *Do not stir.* Once the sugar starts to melt, reduce heat to low. Cook about 5 minutes more or until all of the sugar is melted and golden, stirring as needed with a wooden spoon. Immediately pour the caramelized sugar into a 9×1½-inch round baking pan; using a pot holder, tilt to coat the bottom of the pan evenly. Let stand for 10 minutes.

2. Meanwhile, in a large bowl, beat eggs and egg yolks; beat in whole milk, sweetened condensed milk, and vanilla. Beat with a wire whisk until combined but not foamy.

3. Place the caramel-coated baking pan in a large roasting pan on an oven rack. Pour the egg mixture into the baking pan. Pour boiling water into the roasting pan around the baking pan to a depth of ½ inch.

4. Bake about 35 minutes or until a knife inserted near the center comes out clean. Remove baking pan from water. Cool on a wire rack for 1 hour. Cover and chill for 2 to 24 hours.

5. To serve, loosen edge of flan with a flat metal spatula or knife. Invert a round platter over the flan; turn over baking pan and platter together. Remove baking pan. Scrape any caramelized sugar that remains in the pan onto the flan. Makes 8 servings.

In Spain, Christmas Eve dinner is traditionally served after Midnight Mass. The celebration continues into the early morning hours, because, as the Spanish proverb goes, "This is the *Noche Buena* (the good night); therefore it is not meant for sleep." *Flan,* the hallmark Spanish custard with its silky drape of caramel, graces many a Christmas Eve table. It has also been adapted to the New World—Puerto Ricans use sweet potatoes in their flans.

Orange-Sweet Potato Flan

Orange-Sweet Potato Flans
Flan de Batatas (flawn day bah-TAH-tahz)
Prep: 30 minutes Bake: 40 minutes
Chill: 4 hours

⅔	cup sugar
4	eggs
1	17-ounce can sweet potatoes (vacuum packed), mashed (1¾ cups), or one 15-ounce can pumpkin
1	12-ounce can (1½ cups) evaporated milk
½	cup sugar
¼	cup grated coconut (optional)
2	teaspoons finely shredded orange peel
2	teaspoons vanilla
¾	teaspoon ground allspice

1. Preheat oven to 325°F. To caramelize sugar, in a heavy, large skillet, cook the ⅔ cup sugar over medium-high heat until sugar begins to melt, shaking skillet occasionally to heat sugar evenly. *Do not stir.* Once sugar starts to melt, reduce heat to low. Cook about 5 minutes more or until all sugar is melted and golden, stirring as needed with a wooden spoon.

2. Immediately divide caramelized sugar among eight 6-ounce custard cups. Holding cups with pot holders, quickly tilt cups to evenly coat bottoms. Set aside.

3. In a large bowl, beat eggs; stir in sweet potato or pumpkin, evaporated milk, the ½ cup sugar, the coconut (if desired), orange peel, vanilla, and allspice.

4. Place a large roasting pan on an oven rack. Arrange the custard cups in the pan. Pour sweet potato mixture into cups. Pour boiling water into the roasting pan around the custard cups to a depth of 1 inch.

5. Bake for 40 to 45 minutes or until a knife inserted near the centers comes out clean. Remove cups from water; cool slightly on a wire rack. Cover; chill for 4 to 24 hours.

6. To serve, loosen edges of flans with a flat metal spatula or knife. Invert a dessert plate over each flan; turn over cup and plate together. Remove cups. Scrape any caramelized sugar that remains in cups onto the flans. Makes 8 servings.

Butter Cookie Claws (recipe, page 119),
Cardamom Wreaths (recipe, page 120), and
Currant Cornmeal Diamonds (recipe, page 131)

Global Cookie Exchange

SHARE YOUR HERITAGE with this collection of cookies from around the world. You'll find that almost all your cookie-baking friends have a prized buttery cookie recipe from their homeland—from Scotland's crisp *Shortbread* to Spain's shiny *Mantecados*. And *Macaroons*—are they French or Italian? No need to draw the line—we give recipes inspired by both countries! Recipes and traditions vary from country to country, but this collection shows we all have one thing in common: the love of sharing something sweet from our hands and hearts.

In Norway, these knots are known as *Berlinerkranser,* or Berlin wreaths. As you might guess, Germany also has a version of these wreaths. A similar cookie, *Vanillekranse,* is a Christmas tradition in Denmark; there, cookies are tied with red ribbons and hung on the Christmas tree or in windows.

Butter Knot Cookies

Berlinerkranser (BUR-lin-uhr-kranz-uhr)

Prep: 30 minutes Chill: 1 hour
Bake: 18 minutes per batch Cool: 1 minute

    1   cup butter, softened
    ½   cup sifted powdered sugar
    1   hard-cooked egg yolk
    1   raw egg yolk
    1   teaspoon vanilla
    2¼ cups all-purpose flour
    1   egg white
    2   to 3 tablespoons pearl or coarse sugar

1. In a large bowl, beat butter with an electric mixer on medium to high speed for 30 seconds. Add powdered sugar; beat until combined, scraping side of bowl occasionally.

2. Press hard-cooked egg yolk through a sieve; beat into butter mixture. Beat in raw egg yolk and vanilla. Beat in as much flour as you can with the mixer. Using a wooden spoon, stir in any remaining flour. Cover; chill dough about 1 hour or until firm enough to handle. (Chilling longer may make it too firm.) Preheat oven to 325°F.

3. On a lightly floured surface, roll about *1 tablespoon* of the dough into a 6-inch-long rope. Shape rope into a ring on an ungreased cookie sheet, crossing over ends about 1 inch from endpoints. Repeat with remaining dough, arranging cookies about 2 inches apart on the cookie sheet. Beat with egg white; brush onto cookies. Sprinkle with pearl sugar.

4. Bake for 18 to 20 minutes or until edges are light brown. Cool on cookie sheet for 1 minute. Remove from cookie sheet; cool on a wire rack. Makes about 36 cookies.

Sour Cream Twists
Kringla (KRING-lah)
Prep: 40 minutes Bake: 8 minutes per batch

  3¾ **cups all-purpose flour**
   2 **teaspoons baking powder**
   ½ **teaspoon baking soda**
   ½ **teaspoon salt**
   3 **egg yolks**
  1¼ **cups granulated sugar**
   ½ **cup milk**
   ¼ **cup dairy sour cream**
   1 **tablespoon butter, melted**
   ½ **teaspoon anise extract or vanilla**
Sifted powdered sugar (optional)

1. Lightly grease a cookie sheet; set aside. In a medium bowl, stir together flour, baking powder, baking soda, and salt; set aside.

2. In a large bowl, beat egg yolks slightly; stir in granulated sugar, milk, sour cream, butter, and anise extract until combined. Using a wooden spoon, stir in flour mixture until combined (dough will be stiff). Preheat oven to 350°F.

3. On a lightly floured surface, roll about *1 tablespoon* of the dough into a 5-inch-long rope. On the prepared cookie sheet, shape rope into a ring, crossing over ends about 1 inch from ends. Repeat with remaining dough, arranging cookies about 2 inches apart on the cookie sheet.

4. Bake for 8 to 10 minutes or until golden. Remove from cookie sheet; cool on a wire rack. If desired, sprinkle with powdered sugar. Makes about 60 cookies.

Almond-Coated Cookies
Serinakaker (suhr-een-ah-KAW-kor)
Prep: 25 minutes Chill: 2 to 3 hours
Bake: 8 minutes per batch

  ⅔ **cup butter, softened**
  ½ **cup sugar**
  ¼ **teaspoon baking powder**
  2 **eggs**
  1 **teaspoon vanilla**
  1½ **cups all-purpose flour**
  1 **cup coarsely chopped almonds**

1. Lightly grease a cookie sheet; set aside. In a large bowl, beat butter with an electric mixer on medium to high speed for 30 seconds. Add sugar and baking powder; beat until combined, scraping side of bowl occasionally. Beat in *one* of the eggs and the vanilla until combined. Beat in as much of the flour as you can with the mixer. Using a wooden spoon, stir in any remaining flour. Cover and chill dough for 2 to 3 hours or until firm enough to handle. Preheat oven to 375°F.

2. Beat remaining egg slightly. Shape dough into ¾-inch balls. Roll balls in egg; roll in almonds. Arrange balls 2 inches apart on the prepared cookie sheet. Flatten each ball slightly with a fork.

3. Bake for 8 to 10 minutes or until edges are light brown. Remove from cookie sheet; cool on wire rack. Makes about 48 cookies.

Christmas cookies are highly revered in Norway. In the past, cookies were given as gifts, and the crumbs were believed to possess magical healing powers. It's tradition for families to bake several kinds of cookies for the holiday season (even up to 20!). When you're making that many cookies, it helps to bake them ahead of time. To bake and store any of the cookies in this chapter, layer unfrosted, unfilled cookies between sheets of waxed paper in an airtight container and cover them tightly. Store the cookies at room temperature for up to 3 days. Or layer the cookies in a freezer container and freeze for up to 3 months.

"S" Cookies

Prep: 30 minutes Bake: 8 minutes per batch

> 2½ cups all-purpose flour
> 1 teaspoon baking powder
> 1½ teaspoons ground cinnamon
> ⅔ cup butter, softened
> 1½ cups sugar
> 3 eggs

1. In a small bowl, stir together flour, baking powder, and *1 teaspoon* cinnamon; set aside.

2. In a large bowl, beat butter with an electric mixer on medium to high speed for 30 seconds. Add *1 cup* of the sugar; beat until light and fluffy. Add eggs, one at a time, beating after each addition until combined. Add the flour mixture; beat on low speed until combined. If necessary, cover and chill dough about 1 hour or until firm enough to handle.

3. Lightly grease a cookie sheet; set aside. For coating, in a small bowl, stir together remaining *½ cup* sugar and *½ teaspoon* cinnamon; sprinkle some onto a plate. Preheat oven to 375°F.

4. Drop *1 rounded teaspoon* of the dough into the cinnamon coating; roll into a 3-inch-long rope. On the prepared cookie sheet, shape rope into an "S." Repeat with remaining dough, adding more of the cinnamon coating as needed and leaving about 1 inch space between cookies on cookie sheet.

5. Bake about 8 minutes or until bottoms are golden. Remove from cookie sheet; cool on wire rack. Makes about 60 cookies.

Did you know Finland is Santa's official home? In 1927, the Finnish Broadcasting Company designated a hill in its Lapland territory as the jolly elf's residence. Lucky for Santa, plenty of reindeer thrive in that area. So it seems fitting that Finnish grandmothers shape their cookies into "S" shapes.

Almond Tarts
Sandbakkelse (sahn-BAHK-elz-ah)

Prep: 40 minutes Bake: 10 minutes per batch
Cool: 5 minutes

> ½ cup butter, softened
> ½ cup sugar
> 1 egg
> ½ teaspoon almond extract
> ¼ cup ground almonds
> 1½ cups all-purpose flour
> **Lingonberry jam or orange marmalade**

1. Season 2½-inch sandbakkelse molds, if necessary.* In a large bowl, beat butter with an electric mixer on medium to high speed for 30 seconds. Add sugar; beat until combined, scraping side of bowl occasionally. Add egg and almond extract; beat until combined. Beat in ground almonds and as much of the flour as you can with the mixer. Using a wooden spoon, stir in any remaining flour. If necessary, cover and chill dough about 1 hour or until firm enough to handle. Preheat oven to 350°F.

2. Place *2 to 2½ teaspoons* of the dough in the center of each seasoned sandbakkelse mold. Press dough in an even, very thin layer along the bottom and up the sides, making sure no dough extends over edges of the molds. Place molds on a cookie sheet. (Or press dough into 1¾-inch tart pans or muffin cups.)

3. Bake for 10 to 12 minutes or until edges are firm and light brown. Cool tarts upside down in molds on cookie sheet for 5 minutes. Gently tap bottoms; carefully remove tarts. (Or cool cookies in tart pans or muffin cups for 5 minutes; remove cookies.) Cool on a wire rack. Fill with jam. Makes about 36 tarts.

*Note: To season sandbakkelse molds, grease insides of molds with shortening. Heat in a 300°F oven for 30 minutes. Cool. Wipe out excess shortening. (After use, rinse with water and wipe with paper towels. You won't need to season the molds again.)

Grandmother's Jelly Cookies
Mormor's Syltkakor
(mor-MORZ soolt-KAH-kor)

Prep: 40 minutes Bake: 7 minutes per batch

1	**cup butter, softened**
¾	**cup granulated sugar**
1	**egg**
½	**teaspoon vanilla**
3	**cups all-purpose flour**
1	**slightly beaten egg white**
2	**tablespoons finely chopped almonds and/or pearl sugar**
¼	**cup currant jelly**

1. Lightly grease a cookie sheet; set aside. In a large bowl, beat butter with an electric mixer on medium to high speed for 30 seconds. Add granulated sugar; beat on medium speed until fluffy, scraping side of bowl occasionally. Add egg and vanilla; beat until combined. Beat in as much of the flour as you can with the mixer. Using a wooden spoon, stir in any remaining flour.

2. Preheat oven to 375°F. Divide dough in half. On a lightly floured surface, roll one portion of dough to ⅛-inch thickness. Using a 2½-inch round- or star-shape cutter, cut into rounds or stars. Roll out remaining dough to ⅛-inch thickness; cut with a 2-inch round- or star-shape cookie cutter. Using a ¾- or 1-inch round- or star-shape cutter, cut a circle from center of smaller rounds or stars. Reroll the dough trimmings; cut into shapes.

3. Brush tops of 2-inch shapes with egg white; sprinkle with almonds and/or pearl sugar. Arrange shapes 1 inch apart on prepared cookie sheet.

4. Bake for 7 to 9 minutes or until bottoms are light brown. Remove from cookie sheet; cool on a wire rack.

5. Place a small amount of jelly in centers of the 2½-inch cookies; top with 2-inch cookies, nut and/or sugar sides up, pressing together and showing jelly in center of top cookie. Makes 24 sandwich cookies.

In Swedish, the name *Mormor's Syltkakor* means "grandmother's jelly cookies." Both the jelly cookies and the Norwegian Almond Tarts use jam or jelly to add color and sweetness. We give suggestions for traditional jellies and jams, but you can go ahead and try your favorite flavors.

Grandmother's Jelly Cookies (right) and Almond Tarts (left)

In Sweden, these spicy gingerbread cookies are called *pepparkakor;* popular shapes include hearts, stars, men (and women), goats, and even pigs. Feeling lucky? Tradition holds that if you place the cookie in the palm of your hand and tap it with a knuckle, your wish will come true if the cookie breaks into three pieces.

Gingerbread Cookies
Pepparkakor (pep-par-KAH-kor)
Stand: 45 minutes Prep: 45 minutes
Chill: 2 hours Bake: 5 minutes per batch

- ½ cup sugar
- ½ cup molasses
- ¼ cup shortening
- ¼ cup butter
- 1 beaten egg
- 1 teaspoon ground cinnamon
- ½ teaspoon ground allspice
- ½ teaspoon ground nutmeg
- ½ teaspoon finely shredded orange peel
- ¼ teaspoon salt
- ¼ teaspoon baking soda
- ¼ teaspoon ground cardamom
- ¼ teaspoon ground cloves
- 2½ cups all-purpose flour
- 1 recipe Gingerbread Icing (optional) (above right)
- Red cinnamon candies and/or other small decorative candies (optional)

1. In a medium saucepan, combine sugar, molasses, shortening, and butter. Bring to boiling; reduce heat. Cook and stir for 2 minutes more. Remove from heat; let stand at room temperature for 45 minutes.

2. Add egg, cinnamon, allspice, nutmeg, orange peel, salt, baking soda, cardamom, and cloves to mixture in saucepan; stir to mix. Add flour, a third at a time, stirring well after each addition. Cover and chill dough about 2 hours or until firm enough to handle. (If desired, chill for up to 24 hours.) Preheat oven to 375°F.

3. Lightly grease a cookie sheet; set aside. Divide dough in half. On a well-floured surface, roll each portion to ⅛-inch thickness. Using 3- to 5-inch cutters, cut into desired shapes. Arrange shapes 2 inches apart on prepared cookie sheet.

4. Bake for 5 to 6 minutes or until edges are brown. Remove cookies from cookie sheet; cool on a wire rack.

5. If desired, decorate cooled cookies with Gingerbread Icing and candies. Makes about 64 (3-inch) or 24 (5-inch) cookies.

Gingerbread Icing: In a medium bowl, combine 2 cups sifted powdered sugar, 4 teaspoons meringue powder, and ¼ teaspoon cream of tartar. Add ¼ cup warm water. Beat with an electric mixer on low speed until combined. Beat on high speed for 7 to 10 minutes or until very stiff. Add enough additional water, 1 teaspoon at a time, to make an icing of piping consistency. If desired, tint icing by stirring in desired paste food coloring.

Butter Cookie Claws
Pictured on page 113.
Prep: 20 minutes Chill: 1 hour
Bake: 12 minutes per batch Cool: 1 minute

- 1½ cups all-purpose flour
- 2 tablespoons granulated sugar
- 1 teaspoon baking powder
- 1 cup butter
- ½ cup half-and-half or light cream
- Colored sugar, coarse sugar, or granulated sugar

1. In a large bowl, stir together flour, the 2 tablespoons sugar, and the baking powder. Using a pastry blender, cut in butter until mixture resembles coarse crumbs. Add half-and-half, stirring with a fork until dough clings together. Form dough into a ball. Cover and chill for 1 hour. Preheat oven to 350°F.

2. On a lightly floured surface, roll dough to a 10×8-inch rectangle. Cut into 2×1-inch sticks. Arrange sticks 1 inch apart on an ungreased cookie sheet. Using a small sharp knife, make ½-inch-long slashes on one of the long sides of each cookie, spacing about ½ inch apart. Curve back uncut edges of cookies slightly. Sprinkle with colored, coarse, or granulated sugar.

3. Bake about 12 minutes or until light brown. Cool for 1 minute on cookie sheet. Remove cookies from cookie sheet; cool on a wire rack. Makes 40 cookies.

Cardamom Wreaths
Eier Kringel (AIR kring-guhl)
Pictured on page 113.
Prep: 45 minutes Chill: 2 hours
Bake: 9 minutes per batch

- 3 hard-cooked egg yolks
- ½ cup butter, softened
- ½ cup granulated sugar
- 1 raw egg yolk
- 2 tablespoons milk
- 1 teaspoon finely shredded lemon peel
- ¼ teaspoon salt
- ¼ teaspoon ground cardamom
- 2 cups sifted cake flour or 1¾ cups sifted all-purpose flour
- 1 recipe Powdered Sugar Icing (optional) (below)
- Green food coloring (optional)
- Small red cinnamon candies (optional)

1. Press the hard-cooked egg yolks through a sieve; set aside.

2. In a large bowl, beat butter with an electric mixer on medium to high speed for 30 seconds. Add the ½ cup sugar; beat until light. Add the raw egg yolk, milk, lemon peel, salt, and cardamom; beat on low speed until combined. Beat in the sieved egg yolk and as much of the sifted flour as you can with the mixer. Using a wooden spoon, stir in remaining flour. Form dough into a ball. Cover; chill about 2 hours or until firm enough to roll. Preheat oven to 350°F.

3. Grease a cookie sheet; set aside. Divide dough in half. On a lightly floured surface, roll each portion of dough to ⅛-inch thickness. Using a doughnut-shape cutter, cut into wreaths. Arrange shapes 2 inches apart on prepared cookie sheet. Reroll dough centers with other trimmings.

4. Bake about 9 minutes or until edges are firm and bottoms are light brown. Remove from cookie sheet; cool on a wire rack.

5. If desired, frost with Powdered Sugar Icing. If desired, using a thin paintbrush, apply food coloring onto icing, then garnish with cinnamon candies. Makes 36 cookies.

Powdered Sugar Icing: In a medium bowl, stir together 1 cup sifted powdered sugar, 1 tablespoon milk, and ¼ teaspoon vanilla. Stir in additional milk, 1 teaspoon at a time, to make an icing of spreading consistency.

Peppernuts
Pebbernodder (PEB-ber-noth-er)
Stand: 15 minutes Prep: 1 hour
Chill: 2 hours Bake: 8 minutes per batch

- 1 cup granulated sugar
- 1 cup molasses
- ¼ cup butter
- 2 eggs, slightly beaten
- ½ teaspoon baking powder
- ½ teaspoon baking soda
- ½ teaspoon ground ginger
- ½ teaspoon vanilla
- ¼ teaspoon salt
- ¼ teaspoon ground cinnamon
- ¼ teaspoon ground cardamom
- ¼ teaspoon ground cloves
- ¼ teaspoon anise extract or crushed anise seeds
- ⅛ teaspoon ground black pepper
- 4 cups all-purpose flour
- 1 tablespoon sifted powdered sugar

1. In a large saucepan, combine sugar, molasses, and butter. Bring to boiling, stirring to dissolve sugar. Remove from heat; let stand at room temperature for 15 minutes.

2. Stir eggs, baking powder, baking soda, ginger, vanilla, salt, cinnamon, cardamom, cloves, anise extract or anise seeds, and pepper into molasses mixture. Add flour; stir until combined. Cover and chill about 2 hours or until firm enough to handle. Preheat oven to 375°F.

3. Grease a cookie sheet; set aside. Divide dough into 24 equal portions. Sprinkle a work surface with powdered sugar. On the lightly sugared surface, roll each portion of dough into a ¼-inch-thick rope (about 22 inches long). Cut into ⅜-inch-long pieces. Arrange pieces 1 inch apart on the prepared cookie sheet.

4. Bake about 8 minutes or until bottoms are light brown. Immediately remove from cookie sheet; cool on paper towels. Makes 12 cups (48 servings).

Butter Horns

Prep: 40 minutes Bake: 10 minutes per batch

 2 cups all-purpose flour
 1 teaspoon baking powder
 ¼ teaspoon salt
 ½ cup cold butter
 2 egg yolks
 ¼ cup dairy sour cream
 2 tablespoons water
 ½ teaspoon vanilla
 1 egg white
 ¼ cup granulated sugar
 ¾ cup ground walnuts
 2 tablespoons milk
Sifted powdered sugar (optional)

1. In a large bowl, stir together flour, baking powder, and salt. Using a pastry blender, cut in butter until mixture resembles coarse crumbs. Make a well in the center.

2. In a small bowl, use a fork to beat egg yolks; stir in sour cream, water, and vanilla. Add yolk mixture all at once to flour mixture; stir just until combined. Mix gently with hands until dough forms a ball; set aside.

3. For filling, in a medium bowl, beat egg white with an electric mixer on medium to high speed until soft peaks form (tips curl). Gradually add granulated sugar, beating until stiff peaks form (tips stand straight). Fold in walnuts.

4. Lightly grease a cookie sheet; set aside. Divide dough into four portions. On a lightly floured surface, roll each portion into an 8-inch round. Cut each round into eight wedges, forming 32 wedges. Preheat oven to 400°F.

5. Place *1 rounded teaspoon* of the walnut filling at the wide end of each wedge. Roll up each wedge from wide end to the tip. Arrange roll-ups, tips down, about 1 inch apart on the prepared cookie sheet. Curve each slightly to form a crescent. Brush with milk.

6. Bake for 10 to 12 minutes or until bottoms are golden. Remove from cookie sheet; cool on a wire rack. If desired, sprinkle with powdered sugar. Makes 32 cookies.

Cheese-Filled Butter Cookies

Kolacki (KOH-lah-chee)

Prep: 45 minutes Bake: 18 minutes per batch

 2 cups butter, softened
 ½ cup granulated sugar
 1½ teaspoons vanilla
 4 cups all-purpose flour
 2 tablespoons milk
 ¾ cup large-curd cottage cheese
 1 3-ounce package cream cheese
 1 egg yolk
 ½ cup sifted powdered sugar
Small multicolored decorative candies

1. In a large bowl, beat butter with an electric mixer on medium speed for 30 seconds. Add granulated sugar and *1 teaspoon* vanilla; beat until combined, scraping bowl. Beat in *2 cups* flour and milk. Beat in remaining flour. Cover; set aside.

2. For filling, drain cottage cheese. In a medium bowl, beat cottage cheese, cream cheese, yolk, and remaining *½ teaspoon* vanilla. Beat in powdered sugar until mixed (will not be smooth). Preheat oven to 325°F.

3. Shape into 1-inch balls; arrange 2 inches apart on an ungreased cookie sheet. Using thumb, make an indentation in each ball. Spoon *½ teaspoon* filling into each. Top with candies.

4. Bake for 18 to 20 minutes or until edges are firm but not brown. Remove from sheet; cool on a wire rack. Makes about 84 cookies.

Cheese-Filled Butter Cookies

These sweetly spiced Dutch treats are part of St. Nicholas Eve festivities. They're known as *Speculaas,* from a Latin word meaning mirror. The name comes from the way the dough takes on a mirror image of the mold used for shaping, in this case a windmill. Dutch bakers use other shapes, too.

Spiced Cookie Shapes
Speculaas (SPEK-yoo-lahz)
Prep: 30 minutes Chill: 1 hour
Bake: 8 minutes per batch Cool: 1 minute

- ½ cup butter, softened
- ¾ cup packed brown sugar
- ¾ teaspoon ground cinnamon
- ½ teaspoon baking powder
- ¼ teaspoon ground nutmeg
- ¼ teaspoon ground cloves
- ⅛ teaspoon salt
- 1 egg yolk
- 1 tablespoon milk
- 1⅓ cups all-purpose flour
- 3 tablespoons finely chopped almonds (optional)
- 1 recipe Powdered Sugar Frosting (optional) (right)

1. In a large bowl, beat butter with an electric mixer on medium to high speed for 30 seconds. Add brown sugar, cinnamon, baking powder, nutmeg, cloves, and salt; beat until combined, scraping bowl often. Beat in yolk and milk. Beat in as much flour as you can with the mixer. Using a wooden spoon, stir in any remaining flour and, if desired, nuts. Cover; chill about 1 hour or until firm enough to handle. Preheat oven to 350°F.

2. Lightly grease a cookie sheet; set aside. Lightly oil cookie molds*; press a small amount of dough into an oiled cookie mold. Unmold dough onto the prepared cookie sheet. (If cookie does not unmold easily, tap the mold on the counter to release the dough.) Repeat with remaining dough. Arrange cookies 1 inch apart on the prepared cookie sheet.

3. Bake for 8 to 10 minutes or until edges are golden. Cool cookies on the cookie sheet on a wire rack for 1 minute. Remove from cookie sheet; cool on the wire rack.

4. If desired, decorate cookies with Powdered Sugar Frosting. Makes about 8 (6-inch) or 48 (2- to 2½-inch) cookies.

Powdered Sugar Frosting: In a medium bowl, stir together 1½ cups sifted powdered sugar and 4 teaspoons milk. Stir in additional milk, 1 teaspoon at a time, to make a frosting of piping consistency. Spoon into a piping bag.

*Note: If you do not own cookie molds, on a lightly floured surface, roll half of the dough at a time to ⅛-inch thickness. Using cookie cutters, cut into desired shapes. Arrange cookies 1 inch apart on the prepared cookie sheet. Bake as directed.

Almond Pastry Letters
Banketstaven (ban-ket-STAW-ven)
Prep: 1½ hours Chill: 40 minutes
Bake: 25 minutes per batch

- 4½ cups all-purpose flour
- 1 teaspoon salt
- 2 cups (1 pound) cold butter
- 1 egg
- 1 cup water
- 1 8-ounce can almond paste
- ½ cup granulated sugar
- ½ cup packed brown sugar
- 2 egg whites

1. In a large bowl, stir together flour and salt. Cut butter into ½-inch-thick slices. Stir butter into flour mixture, coating each butter piece to separate pieces. (Butter will be in large chunks.)

2. In a small bowl, combine egg and water. Add egg mixture all at once to flour mixture; mix quickly. (Butter will still be in pieces and flour will not be completely moistened.)

3. On a lightly floured surface, knead dough 10 times, pressing to form a ball. Shape into a rectangle (will have dry areas). Flatten slightly.

4. On a well-floured surface, roll dough into a 15×10-inch rectangle. Fold the two short sides to meet in the center; fold dough in half crosswise to form four layers and a 7×5-inch rectangle. Repeat rolling and folding. Cover dough with plastic wrap; chill for 20 minutes. Repeat rolling and folding twice more; chill for 20 minutes more.

5. Meanwhile, for filling, in a medium bowl, combine almond paste, the ½ cup granulated sugar, the brown sugar, and egg whites; beat with an electric mixer on medium speed until smooth. Cover; chill 20 minutes. Preheat oven to 375°F.

6. Cut dough crosswise into four portions. Roll *one* portion into a 12×10-inch rectangle. (Keep remaining portions in refrigerator.) Cut into four 10×3-inch strips. Spread *1 rounded tablespoon* of filling down the center of each strip. Roll up each strip lengthwise around filling. Brush seams with milk; pinch to seal. Arrange, seam sides down, on an ungreased cookie sheet, shaping each into an "S" or other letter shape. Top with additional milk and granulated sugar. Repeat with remaining dough and filling.

7. Bake 25 to 30 minutes or until golden. Remove from sheet; cool on a rack. Makes 16.

Cinnamon-Almond Bars
Jan Hagels (YAWN hay-guhls)
Pictured on page 125.
Prep: 15 minutes Bake: 15 minutes
Stand: 5 minutes

- 1 cup butter, softened
- ¾ cup granulated sugar
- 1 teaspoon ground cinnamon
- ¼ teaspoon baking soda
- 1 egg yolk
- 2 cups all-purpose flour
- 1 egg white
- ½ cup sliced almonds
- Sifted powdered sugar (optional)

1. Grease a 15×10×1-inch baking pan; set pan aside. In a large bowl, beat butter with an electric mixer on medium to high speed for 30 seconds. Add granulated sugar, cinnamon, and baking soda; beat until combined, scraping the side of the bowl occasionally. Beat in egg yolk until combined. Beat or stir in flour until combined. Preheat oven to 350°F.

2. Using lightly floured hands, pat dough evenly into the prepared pan. Beat egg white slightly; brush onto dough. Sprinkle with almonds; lightly press almonds into dough.

3. Bake for 15 to 18 minutes or until golden. Remove from oven; let stand for 5 minutes in pan. Cut into bars. Remove from pan; cool on a wire rack. If desired, sprinkle with powdered sugar. Makes 36 bars.

Christmas comes early in Holland! Traditionally, on December 5, the Dutch celebrate St. Nicholas (*Sinterklass*) Eve. On that day, they exchange cleverly wrapped gifts, often with a rhyme telling a humorous story about the recipient. Almond Pastry Letters (pastries filled with almond paste and shaped into initial letters) are often used as place cards on the holiday table.

Spiced Meringue Stars
Zimsterne (ZIM-stehr-nah)
Prep: 30 minutes Stand: 1 hour
Bake: 10 minutes per batch

  2 **egg whites**
1½ **cups ground almonds, toasted**
 ¾ **cup ground hazelnuts (filberts), toasted**
  2 **tablespoons all-purpose flour**
  1 **teaspoon ground cinnamon**
 ¼ **teaspoon ground nutmeg**
  1 **cup granulated sugar**
Sifted powdered sugar (optional)

1. In a large bowl, let egg whites stand at room temperature for 30 minutes. Meanwhile, grease a large cookie sheet; set aside.

2. In a medium bowl, stir together almonds, hazelnuts, flour, cinnamon, and nutmeg; set aside.

3. In a small bowl, beat egg whites with an electric mixer on medium speed until soft peaks form (tips curl). Gradually add granulated sugar, *1 tablespoon* at a time, beating on high speed until stiff peaks form (tips stand straight) and sugar is almost dissolved. Fold nut mixture into beaten egg whites. Cover and let stand for 30 minutes. Preheat oven to 325°F.

4. Sprinkle powdered sugar onto work surface. On the sugared surface, roll dough to ¼-inch thickness. Using a floured 2- to 2¼-inch star-shape cookie cutter, cut out dough. Arrange about 1 inch apart on the prepared cookie sheet.

5. Bake about 10 minutes or until light brown and crisp. Remove from cookie sheet; cool on a wire rack. If desired, sprinkle with powdered sugar. Makes about 32 cookies.

In Germany, the weeks before Christmas see a flurry of preparation, with so much baking that cooks divide it into two stages—big baking (when tortes and larger goods are baked), and small baking (when small sweets, such as cookies, are baked). *Springerle,* nut crescents, and meringue stars are just a few of the popular German cookies baked during the small baking stage.

Spiced Citrus Honey Sticks
Leckerli (LEK-uhr-lee)
Prep: 35 minutes Bake: 10 minutes per batch

2½ **cups all-purpose flour**
  1 **cup sugar**
  1 **cup finely chopped almonds**
 ¼ **cup candied orange peel, finely chopped**
 ¼ **cup candied lemon peel, finely chopped**
  1 **teaspoon baking powder**
  1 **teaspoon ground cinnamon**
 ½ **teaspoon ground nutmeg**
 ¼ **teaspoon ground cloves**
 ¾ **cup honey**
  2 **tablespoons kirsch or brandy**
  1 **beaten egg**
  1 **recipe Citrus Glaze (below)**

1. Grease a large cookie sheet; set aside. In a large bowl, stir together flour, sugar, almonds, orange peel, lemon peel, baking powder, cinnamon, nutmeg, and cloves. Make a well in the center of the flour mixture. Add honey, kirsch or brandy, and egg. Stir and knead dough, forming it into a ball. Preheat oven to 350°F.

2. Divide dough in half. On a lightly floured surface, roll each portion of dough to ¼-inch thickness. Cut dough into 5×1-inch strips. Arrange strips 1 inch apart on the prepared cookie sheet.

3. Bake about 10 minutes or until golden. Transfer cookies to a wire rack. Brush tops of warm cookies with Citrus Glaze. Cool on a wire rack. Makes about 30 cookies.

Citrus Glaze: In a small bowl, stir together 1 cup sifted powdered sugar, ½ teaspoon finely shredded lemon peel or orange peel, and 2 teaspoons lemon juice or orange juice. Add enough water (2 to 3 teaspoons) to make an icing of glazing consistency.

Anise Stamped Cookies
Springerle (SPRING-*uhr-lee*)
Prep: 1 hour Stand: 8 hours
Bake: 20 minutes per batch Store: 3 days

3½ cups all-purpose flour
1 teaspoon baking soda
4 eggs
1 16-ounce package powdered sugar, sifted (about 4¾ cups)
20 drops oil of anise (about ¼ teaspoon)
Crushed anise seeds
Cold water

1. In a small bowl, stir together flour and baking soda; set aside.

2. In a large bowl, beat eggs with an electric mixer on high speed for 15 minutes or until thick and lemon colored. Gradually add powdered sugar, beating on low speed until combined. Beat on high speed for 15 minutes more or until soft peaks form.

3. Add oil of anise. Beat in as much of the flour mixture as you can with the mixer (the dough will be thick). Using a wooden spoon, stir in any remaining flour mixture. Cover; let stand about 15 minutes for easier handling.

4. Divide dough into three portions. Roll *one* portion to ¼-inch thickness (keep remaining dough covered). Let stand for 1 minute.

5. Sprinkle a springerle mold or rolling pin with additional flour; press or roll into dough to make a clear design. Using a knife, cut cookies apart. Arrange on a lightly floured surface. Repeat with remaining dough. Cover loosely with a clean towel; let stand at room temperature for 8 to 12 hours. Preheat oven to 300°F.

6. Lightly grease a cookie sheet; sprinkle with 1½ to 2 teaspoons crushed anise seeds. Brush excess flour from cookies. Using your finger or a pastry brush, lightly brush the bottom of each cookie with cold water. Arrange cookies on the prepared cookie sheet.

7. Bake about 20 minutes or until light brown. Remove from cookie sheet; cool on wire rack. Store in a tightly covered container for at least 3 days before serving. Makes 72 (2-inch) cookies.

Hazelnut Crescents
Prep: 25 minutes Bake: 12 minutes per batch

1 cup butter, softened
½ cup granulated sugar
1 teaspoon vanilla
2 cups all-purpose flour
½ cup ground hazelnuts (filberts)
Sifted powdered sugar

1. In a large bowl, beat butter, granulated sugar, and vanilla with an electric mixer on high speed until fluffy. Add flour and nuts; beat until mixed. Preheat oven to 325°F.

2. Using about 2 *teaspoons* dough for each, form into crescent shapes, tapering ends. Arrange 1 inch apart on ungreased cookie sheet.

3. Bake for 12 to 15 minutes or until bottoms are light brown. Remove from cookie sheet; cool on a wire rack. Sprinkle with powdered sugar. Makes about 60 crescents.

Cinnamon-Almond Bars (recipe, page 123) and Spiced Citrus Honey Sticks

Brandy Snaps

Prep: 40 minutes Bake: 9 minutes per batch
Cool: 1 minute

- ¾ **cup all-purpose flour**
- ½ **teaspoon ground ginger**
- ½ **cup sugar**
- ½ **cup butter**
- ⅓ **cup golden syrup* or dark-colored corn syrup**
- 1 **tablespoon brandy**

1. Line a cookie sheet with foil; lightly grease foil. Grease a metal cone or the handle of a wooden spoon. Set aside.

2. In a small bowl, stir together flour and ginger; set aside. Preheat oven to 350°F.

3. In a medium saucepan, combine sugar, butter, and syrup. Cook and stir over low heat until butter is melted; remove from heat. Stir flour mixture into butter mixture. Stir in brandy.

4. Drop batter by rounded teaspoons 3 to 4 inches apart onto the prepared cookie sheet, allowing 2 or 3 cookies per sheet. Bake for 9 to 10 minutes or until bubbly and golden brown.

5. Cool cookies on cookie sheet for 1 to 2 minutes or just until set. Quickly invert cookies onto a cool cookie sheet; wrap each cookie around the prepared metal cone or wooden spoon handle. When cookie is set, slide cookie off cone or spoon; cool on a wire rack. Repeat with remaining batter. Makes about 30 cookies.

*Note: Golden syrup, popular in England, is available in specialty stores and supermarkets.

126

Citrus Shortbread

Prep: 15 minutes Bake: 25 minutes
Cool: 5 minutes

> 1¼ cups all-purpose flour
> 3 tablespoons sugar
> 1 teaspoon finely shredded orange peel
> ½ cup butter

1. Preheat oven to 325°F. In a medium bowl, stir together flour, sugar, and peel. Using a pastry blender, cut in butter until mixture resembles coarse crumbs and starts to cling together. Form into a ball; knead until smooth.

2. On an ungreased cookie sheet, pat or roll dough into an 8-inch round. Using your fingers, press to make a scalloped edge. Cut the round into 16 wedges, but do not separate. Prick each wedge with a fork.

3. Bake for 25 to 30 minutes or until the center is set. While warm, cut circle into wedges again. Cool on the cookie sheet for 5 minutes. Remove cookies from cookie sheet; cool on a wire rack. Makes 16 wedges.

Oatmeal Citrus Shortbread: Prepare Citrus Shortbread as directed, except reduce flour to 1 cup. After cutting in butter, stir in ⅓ cup quick-cooking rolled oats. Continue as directed.

Almond Balls

Kourabiedes (koo-rah-bee-YAY-dehs)

Prep: 40 minutes Bake: 15 minutes

> 1 cup butter, softened
> ⅔ cup sifted powdered sugar
> ½ teaspoon baking powder
> 1 egg yolk
> 2 tablespoons brandy or orange juice
> ½ teaspoon vanilla
> 2¼ cups all-purpose flour
> ⅔ cup finely chopped almonds or walnuts, toasted
> Whole cloves (optional)
> Sifted powdered sugar

1. In a large bowl, beat butter with an electric mixer on medium to high speed for 30 seconds. Add the ⅔ cup powdered sugar and the baking powder; beat until combined, scraping side of bowl occasionally.

2. Beat in egg yolk, brandy or orange juice, and vanilla until combined. Using a wooden spoon, stir in flour and nuts. Preheat oven to 325°F.

3. Shape dough into 1-inch balls. Arrange balls 2 inches apart on an ungreased cookie sheet. If desired, insert a whole clove, stem end first, into the center of each cookie.

4. Bake for 15 to 20 minutes or until bottoms are light brown. Remove from cookie sheet; cool on wire rack. Sprinkle with powdered sugar. Makes about 52 cookies.

Coconut Macaroons

Prep: 15 minutes Bake: 20 minutes per batch

> 2 egg whites
> ½ teaspoon vanilla
> ⅔ cup sugar
> 1 3½-ounce can (1⅓ cups) flaked coconut

1. Preheat oven to 325°F. Lightly grease a cookie sheet; set aside. In a medium bowl, beat egg whites and vanilla with an electric mixer on high speed until soft peaks form. Gradually add sugar, about 1 *tablespoon* at a time, beating until stiff peaks form (tips stand straight). Fold in coconut.

2. Drop dough by rounded teaspoons 2 inches apart onto the prepared cookie sheet. Bake about 20 minutes or until edges are light brown. Remove from cookie sheet; cool on a wire rack. Makes about 30 cookies.

Lemon Coconut Macaroons: Prepare Coconut Macaroons as directed, except substitute 1 tablespoon lemon juice for the vanilla and add 1 teaspoon finely shredded lemon peel.

> **Although shortbread is considered to be Scottish,** many countries bake shortbreadlike cookies during the holidays. For example, Greeks bake buttery *Kourabiedes* for both Christmas and Epiphany. Greek cooks traditionally top each of these melt-in-your-mouth almond balls with a whole clove. The clove represents the spices brought to the Christ child by the Three Kings. However, think of the strongly flavored spice as a decoration and remove it before eating.

Citrus Fig Spirals

Prep: 35 minutes Chill: 5 hours
Bake: 9 minutes per batch

⅓ cup butter, softened
1 cup sugar
½ teaspoon baking powder
1 egg
3 tablespoons milk
½ teaspoon vanilla
2½ cups all-purpose flour
1 cup finely snipped dried figs
⅓ cup orange marmalade
¼ cup orange juice

1. In a large bowl, beat butter with an electric mixer on medium to high speed for 30 seconds. Add sugar and baking powder; beat until combined, scraping side of bowl occasionally. Beat in egg, milk, and vanilla until combined. Beat in as much of the flour as you can with the mixer. Using a wooden spoon, stir in any remaining flour. Cover; chill about 1 hour or until firm enough to handle.

2. Meanwhile, for filling, in a small saucepan, combine figs, marmalade, and orange juice. Cook and stir just until boiling; remove from heat. Set aside to cool.

3. Divide dough in half. Roll each portion of dough between two pieces of plastic wrap into 10×8-inch rectangles. Spread filling onto each dough rectangle to within ½ inch of edges. Starting with a short side, carefully roll up dough rectangles into spirals, using the plastic wrap to lift and guide the roll. Moisten edges; pinch to seal. Wrap in plastic wrap. Chill about 4 hours or until firm enough to slice. (If desired, chill for up to 24 hours.) Preheat oven to 375°F.

4. Line a large cookie sheet with foil; grease foil. Cut rolls into ¼-inch-thick slices. Arrange slices 2 inches apart on the prepared cookie sheet.

5. Bake for 9 to 11 minutes or until edges are firm and bottoms are light brown. Remove from the cookie sheet; cool on a wire rack. Makes about 60 cookies.

Almond Macaroons
Amaretti (am-ah-REHT-tee)

Prep: 20 minutes Bake: 12 minutes per batch
Stand: 30 minutes per batch

2 egg whites
1 tablespoon amaretto or ¼ teaspoon almond extract
½ teaspoon vanilla
1 cup sifted powdered sugar
1¼ cups ground almonds

1. Preheat oven to 300°F. Line a cookie sheet with parchment paper; set aside. In a medium bowl, combine egg whites, amaretto or almond extract, and vanilla; beat with an electric mixer on medium speed until foamy. Gradually beat in sugar. Beat on high speed for 4 to 5 minutes or until very light and soft peaks form (tips curl). Fold in almonds.

2. Drop almond mixture from a rounded teaspoon 2 inches apart onto the prepared cookie sheet. (Cover and chill remaining batter in the refrigerator while first batch bakes and dries.)

3. Bake for 12 minutes. Turn off oven; leave door closed. Let cookies dry in the oven for 30 minutes.

4. Remove cookies from cookie sheet; cool on wire rack. Line cookie sheet with new parchment paper. Repeat with remaining batter. Makes about 24 cookies.

Citrus Fig Spirals

Currant Cornmeal Diamonds
Zaletti (zah-LEHT-tee)

Pictured on page 113.
Stand: 30 minutes Prep: 1 hour
Chill: 3 hours Bake: 6 minutes per batch

- ¾ cup dried currants
- 2 tablespoons dark rum
- ⅔ cup butter, softened
- ⅔ cup granulated sugar
- 1 teaspoon baking powder
- ¼ teaspoon salt
- 1 egg
- 2 teaspoons finely shredded orange peel
- ½ cup yellow cornmeal
- 1½ cups all-purpose flour
- Sifted powdered sugar (optional)

1. In a small bowl, combine currants and rum; cover and let stand for 30 minutes.

2. In a large bowl, beat butter with an electric mixer on medium to high speed for 30 seconds. Add granulated sugar, baking powder, and salt; beat until combined, scraping side of bowl occasionally. Beat in egg and orange peel. Beat in cornmeal and as much of the flour as you can with the mixer. Using a wooden spoon, stir in any remaining flour. Stir in currant mixture. Cover and chill about 3 hours or until dough is firm enough to handle. (If desired, chill for up to 24 hours.) Preheat oven to 375°F.

3. Divide dough in half. On a lightly floured surface, roll each portion into a 12×8-inch rectangle. Using a knife, cut diagonally into 3×1¼-inch diamond shapes. Arrange diamonds 1 inch apart on an ungreased cookie sheet.

4. Bake for 6 to 8 minutes or until edges are light brown. Remove from cookie sheet; cool on a wire rack. If desired, sprinkle with powdered sugar. Makes about 54 cookies.

Cherry-Almond Biscotti
Buon Natale Biscotti (bon nah-TAH-lee)

Prep: 35 minutes Bake: 40 minutes
Cool: 1 hour

- ½ cup butter, softened
- 1 cup sugar
- 2½ teaspoons baking powder
- 2 eggs
- 1 egg yolk
- 1 tablespoon finely shredded orange peel
- 3 cups all-purpose flour
- ¾ cup chopped candied red cherries
- ¾ cup chopped candied green cherries
- ½ cup coarsely chopped almonds, toasted
- 1 egg white, slightly beaten
- 1 teaspoon water
- 2 tablespoons sugar

1. Lightly grease a cookie sheet; set aside. In a large bowl, beat butter with an electric mixer on medium to high speed for 30 seconds. Add the 1 cup sugar and the baking powder; beat until combined. Beat in eggs, egg yolk, and orange peel until combined. Beat in as much of the flour as you can with the mixer. Using a wooden spoon, stir in any remaining flour, the candied cherries, and almonds. Preheat oven to 375°F.

2. Divide dough in half. Shape each portion into a 14-inch-long loaf. Place loaves 3 inches apart on the prepared cookie sheet. Flatten each loaf slightly to a 2-inch width. In a small bowl, stir together egg white and water; brush onto loaves. Sprinkle with the 2 tablespoons sugar.

3. Bake for 20 to 25 minutes or until light brown. Cool loaves on cookie sheet about 1 hour or until completely cool.

4. Preheat oven to 325°F. Transfer cooled loaves to a cutting board. Using a serrated knife, cut each loaf diagonally into ½-inch-thick slices. Arrange slices, cut sides down, on the cookie sheet. Bake for 10 minutes.

5. Turn slices to the other cut sides; bake about 10 minutes more or until dry and crisp. Remove from cookie sheet; cool on a wire rack. Makes about 40 biscotti.

Glazed Lemon-Almond Cookies
Mantecados (mahn-tay-CAW-dohz)
Prep: 30 minutes Chill: 1 hour
Bake: 8 minutes per batch Cool: 2 minutes

- 1 cup butter, softened
- 1 cup granulated sugar
- 2 cups all-purpose flour
- ½ cup ground almonds
- 1 tablespoon finely shredded lemon peel
- 1 egg
- 1 teaspoon lemon juice
- Colored sugar (optional)

1. In a large bowl, beat butter with an electric mixer on medium to high speed for 30 seconds. Add the 1 cup sugar; beat until combined, scraping side of bowl occasionally. Beat in as much of the flour as you can with the mixer. Using a wooden spoon, stir in almonds, lemon peel, and any remaining flour. (Mixture may seem dry at first. If necessary, knead gently with your hands until mixture clings together.) Cover and chill about 1 hour or until firm enough to handle. Preheat oven to 350°F.

2. Divide dough into three portions. On a lightly floured surface, roll each portion of dough to ⅛- to ¼-inch thickness. Using floured 2-inch cookie cutters, cut into desired shapes.

3. Arrange cutouts 1 inch apart on an ungreased cookie sheet. In a small bowl, stir together egg and lemon juice; brush onto cookies. If desired, sprinkle with colored sugar.

4. Bake for 8 to 10 minutes or until edges are light brown. Cool on a cookie sheet for 2 minutes. Remove from cookie sheet; cool on a wire rack. Makes about 60 cookies.

Anise Sugar Cookies
Bizcochitos (biz-koh-CHEE-tohs)
Prep: 40 minutes Bake: 10 minutes per batch

- 3 cups all-purpose flour
- 1½ teaspoons baking powder
- ½ teaspoon salt
- 1 cup shortening, lard, or butter, softened
- ¾ cup sugar
- 1 egg
- 1 tablespoon anise seeds, toasted*
- ¼ cup brandy or milk
- 1 recipe Egg Yolk Paint (optional) (below)

1. In a medium bowl, stir together flour, baking powder, and salt; set aside.

2. In a large bowl, beat shortening, sugar, egg, and anise seeds with an electric mixer on medium to high speed until fluffy. Gradually beat in brandy or milk and as much of the flour mixture as you can with the mixer. Using a wooden spoon, stir in any remaining flour mixture.

3. Divide dough in half. On a lightly floured surface, roll each portion of dough to ¼-inch thickness. Using 2½-inch flower-, leaf-, or other shape cookie cutters, cut dough into shapes. Preheat oven to 350°F.

4. Arrange cutouts 2 inches apart on an ungreased cookie sheet. If desired, brush red and yellow Egg Yolk Paint onto flower shapes to resemble poinsettias. Brush green Egg Yolk Paint onto leaf shapes.

5. Bake for 10 to 12 minutes or until edges are golden. Remove from cookie sheet; cool on a wire rack. Makes about 48 cookies.

Egg Yolk Paint: To make red, yellow, and green paints, in each of 3 small bowls, combine 1 egg yolk and 1 teaspoon water. Add 1 to 2 drops red food coloring to first bowl, 1 to 2 drops yellow food coloring to the second bowl, and 1 to 2 drops green food coloring to the third bowl.

*Note: Toast anise seeds in a dry skillet over medium heat until fragrant. Remove from skillet immediately so they don't burn.

Glazed Lemon-Almond Cookies
and Anise Sugar Cookies

Mexico's cookies have roots in Spain. For example, *Mantecados* are a Christmas treat in both counties. (*Manteca* is the word for fat, lard, or butter in Spanish, perfect for these buttery egg-yolk-glazed treats.) Anise-flavored *bizcochitos* are baked for many special occasions in Mexico, but on Christmas day, iris-shaped *bizcochitos* are given to children after church. Red and green poinsettias make a colorful floral option.

Old-World Gifts

GIVING GIFTS is a beloved holiday custom, symbolic of the Magi, or Three Kings, who bestowed precious gifts upon the Christ child. In Latin countries, children wait until the Epiphany to receive their presents, in honor of the Kings. In Holland, St. Nicholas brings gifts on St. Nicholas Eve. But in most countries, gifts appear on Christmas Eve or Christmas Day, brought under the guise of the French Papa Noel, the British Father Christmas, the Scandinavian Yule Elf, or Santa Claus. When you exchange gifts doesn't really matter; it's the delight that counts—and these delicious homemade gifts assure just that.

From left to right: Thyme-and-Orange Vinegar (page 141), Cranberry Vodka (page 141), and Lemon-Honey Jelly (page 138)

Happy Holidays!

Chocolate-Coconut Scones

Prep: 20 minutes **Bake:** 20 minutes
Cool: 5 minutes

- 2 cups all-purpose flour
- 3 tablespoons granulated sugar
- 2 teaspoons baking powder
- ¼ teaspoon salt
- 6 tablespoons butter
- 1 egg
- ½ cup purchased unsweetened coconut milk or milk
- ⅓ cup shredded coconut
- ⅓ cup miniature semisweet chocolate pieces
- **Milk (optional)**
- **Coarse sugar (optional)**

1. Preheat oven to 400°F. Lightly grease a baking sheet; set aside. In a large bowl, stir together flour, the 3 tablespoons sugar, the baking powder, and salt. Using a pastry blender, cut in butter until mixture resembles coarse crumbs. Make a well in center of flour mixture; set aside.

2. In a small bowl, use a fork to beat egg; stir in coconut milk, coconut, and chocolate pieces. Add egg mixture all at once to flour mixture. Stir just until moistened.

3. Turn out dough onto a lightly floured surface. Gently knead by folding and pressing dough for 10 to 12 strokes or until nearly smooth. On the prepared baking sheet, pat or lightly roll dough into a 7-inch round. Cut into eight wedges; do not separate. If desired, brush with milk; sprinkle with coarse sugar.

4. Bake for 20 to 25 minutes or until golden. Remove scones from the baking sheet; cool on a wire rack for 5 minutes. Separate into wedges; serve scones warm or cool them for gift-giving. Makes 8 scones.

Fruit Scones: Prepare Chocolate-Coconut Scones as directed, except use milk instead of coconut milk and omit coconut and chocolate pieces. Stir ½ cup dried blueberries, raisins, currants, or snipped dried cherries or cranberries into flour mixture.

Chocolate-Coconut Scones

If you're baking food gifts for holidays, why not make them ahead? Cool breads, cakes, and cookies without any frosting, filling, or syrup. Place in airtight containers and store in a cool, dry place for up to three days. (Or place in layers in freezer containers and freeze for up to three months.) Before giving, fill, frost, or coat your baked treasures. Then find a pretty plate or container and wrap each gift in plastic wrap. Decorate with ribbon or garland and add a gift tag with serving suggestions.

Miniature Amaretto Cakes

Stand: 30 minutes **Prep:** 45 minutes
Bake: 20 minutes **Cool:** 10 minutes

- ¾ cup butter
- 3 eggs
- 1½ cups all-purpose flour
- 1 teaspoon baking powder
- ¼ teaspoon ground nutmeg
- ¾ cup sugar
- ¼ cup amaretto
- 1 teaspoon finely shredded lemon peel or orange peel
- ½ teaspoon vanilla
- 1 recipe Amaretto Syrup (below)

Miniature Amaretto Cakes

1. Let the butter and eggs stand at room temperature for 30 minutes. Generously grease and flour six 4-inch fluted tube pans or one 6-cup fluted tube pan. In a small bowl, stir together flour, baking powder, and nutmeg. Set aside.

2. Preheat oven to 325°F. In a large bowl, beat butter with an electric mixer on medium speed for 30 seconds. Add sugar, *2 tablespoons* at a time, beating on medium-high speed about 6 minutes or until light and fluffy, scraping bowl often.

3. Beat in amaretto, peel, and vanilla. Add eggs, *one* at a time, beating for 1 minute after each addition and scraping bowl often. Gradually add flour mixture, beating on medium-low speed just until combined. Pour into prepared pan(s).

4. Bake until a wooden toothpick inserted near the center(s) comes out clean. (Allow 20 to 25 minutes for the 4-inch pans or 40 to 45 minutes for the 6-cup pan.) Cool in pan(s) on wire rack(s) for 10 minutes. Remove from pan(s); cool on wire rack(s).

5. Place cake(s) on wire racks over a large tray. Prick tops and sides of each cake with a fork. Spoon Amaretto Syrup onto cake(s), spooning up syrup on tray. Cool cake(s) on wire rack(s). Makes 1 large or 4 small cakes (24 servings).

Amaretto Syrup: In a medium saucepan, combine ⅓ cup granulated sugar, ¼ cup water, 2 tablespoons brown sugar, and 2 tablespoons light-colored corn syrup. Cook and stir over medium heat until bubbly and most of the sugar is dissolved; remove from heat. Stir in ½ cup amaretto. Cool for 5 minutes.

Eggnog Quick Bread

Prep: 20 minutes **Bake:** 45 minutes
Cool: 10 minutes

- 2¼ cups all-purpose flour
- 2 teaspoons baking powder
- ¼ teaspoon salt
- ¼ teaspoon ground nutmeg
- 2 eggs
- 1 cup sugar
- 1 cup dairy eggnog
- ½ cup butter, melted
- 1 teaspoon vanilla
- ½ teaspoon rum extract (optional)

1. Preheat oven to 350°F. Grease bottom(s) and ½ inch up the sides of one 9×5×3-inch, two 7½×3½×2-inch, or four 4½×2½×1½-inch loaf pans; set aside. In a large bowl, stir together flour, baking powder, salt, and nutmeg. Make a well in the center; set aside.

2. In a small bowl, beat eggs; stir in sugar, eggnog, butter, vanilla, and, if desired, rum extract. Add to flour mixture. Stir just until moistened (batter should be lumpy). Spoon into prepared pan(s).

3. Bake until a wooden toothpick inserted near center(s) comes out clean. (Allow 45 to 50 minutes for the 9×5-inch loaf, 40 to 45 minutes for the 7½×3½-inch loaves, or 35 to 40 minutes for the 4½×2½-inch loaves.) Cool in pan(s) on wire rack(s) for 10 minutes. Remove from pan(s); cool on rack(s). Wrap; store overnight. Makes 1 large, 2 medium, or 4 small loaves (16 servings).

Hugs and Kisses Spritz

Nougat
Turrón (TOO-ron)
Stand: 30 minutes Prep: 40 minutes
Cook: 40 minutes

- 2 egg whites
- Cornstarch
- 1½ cups granulated sugar
- 1 tablespoon cornstarch
- ¼ teaspoon ground coriander or ground cinnamon
- ¾ cup light-colored corn syrup
- ½ cup water
- ¼ cup honey
- 1 teaspoon vanilla
- ½ cup slivered almonds, toasted
- ½ cup chopped hazelnuts, toasted
- Powdered sugar

Hugs and Kisses Spritz
Prep: 25 minutes Bake: 8 minutes per batch

- 1½ cups butter, softened
- 1 cup granulated sugar
- 1 teaspoon baking powder
- 1 egg
- 1 teaspoon vanilla
- ¼ teaspoon almond extract (optional)
- 3½ cups all-purpose flour
- Coarse or colored sugar (optional)

1. Preheat oven to 375°F. In a large bowl, beat butter with an electric mixer on medium to high speed for 30 seconds. Add granulated sugar and baking powder; beat until combined, scraping side of bowl. Beat in egg, vanilla, and, if desired, almond extract until combined. Beat in as much of the flour as you can with the mixer. Using a wooden spoon, stir in any remaining flour.

2. Using a small star template, push unchilled dough through a cookie press onto an ungreased cookie sheet, making 5-inch-long ropes. To make "X"s, cut ropes in half and cross. To make "O"s, shape ropes into circles. If desired, sprinkle with coarse or colored sugar.

3. Bake for 8 to 10 minutes or until edges are firm but not brown. Remove from cookie sheet; cool on a wire rack. Makes about 84 cookies.

1. Let egg whites stand at room temperature for 30 minutes. Line a 9×9×2-inch baking pan with foil, extending foil over edges. Butter the foil; sprinkle with a little cornstarch. Set aside.

2. In a heavy 2-quart saucepan, combine granulated sugar, 1 tablespoon cornstarch, and coriander. Stir in syrup, water, and honey. Cook and stir over medium-high heat until mixture boils and sugar is dissolved (5 to 7 minutes). Avoid splashing mixture onto side of pan.

3. Clip a candy thermometer to side of pan. Reduce heat to medium; continue boiling at a moderate, steady rate over entire surface, stirring occasionally, until thermometer registers 286°F, soft-crack stage (40 to 45 minutes). (Adjust heat as necessary to maintain a steady boil.)

4. Remove from heat; remove thermometer. In a large bowl, beat egg whites with a sturdy, freestanding electric mixer on medium speed until stiff peaks form (tips stand straight).

5. Gradually pour hot mixture in a thin stream (slightly less than ⅛-inch diameter) over egg whites, beating on high speed and scraping the side of the bowl occasionally (about 3 minutes).

6. Add vanilla. Continue beating with the electric mixer on high speed, scraping the side of the bowl occasionally, until candy becomes very thick and just starts to loss its gloss (5 to 6 minutes). (When beaters are lifted, mixture should fall in a ribbon that mounds on itself, then slowly disappears into the remaining mixture.)

136

7. Immediately stir in nuts. Quickly turn nougat mixture into the prepared pan. Using a cornstarch-dipped knife, score warm nougat into 2×¾-inch pieces. When candy is firm, use foil to lift it out of pan; cut candy into pieces. Coat each piece lightly with powdered sugar; wrap in plastic wrap. Makes about 48 pieces.

Make-Ahead Tip: Prepare Nougat as directed. Place candy in an airtight container; cover. Store at room temperature for up to 2 weeks.

Liqueur Chocolate Truffles
Start to finish: 30 minutes

- ½ **cup butter, softened**
- ½ **cup ground or finely chopped nuts (such as almonds, pecans, or walnuts), toasted**
- ¼ **cup unsweetened cocoa powder**
- ¼ **cup orange, raspberry, coffee, cherry, or coconut liqueur**
- 4¾ **cups sifted powdered sugar**

1. In a large bowl, combine butter, nuts, cocoa powder, and desired liqueur; beat with an electric mixer on medium speed until combined.

2. Gradually add powdered sugar, beating until combined. (The mixture will be stiff. If it is too dry, beat in enough additional liqueur, *1 teaspoon* at a time, to make of rolling consistency.)

3. Place mixture between two sheets of waxed paper; roll to ½-inch thickness. Using small (1¼ to 1½-inch) cookie cutters, cut the dough into desired shapes. (Roll the trimmings into 1-inch balls; if desired, top each with a piece of nut.) Cover; chill in the refrigerator until serving time. Makes about 1½ pounds (about 60 pieces).

Make-Ahead Tip: Prepare Liqueur Chocolate Truffles as directed. In an airtight container, layer candy between sheets of waxed paper; cover. Store in the refrigerator for up to 1 week.

Almond Paste Candy
Marzipan (MAHR-zih-pan)
Start to finish: 1 hour

- 1 **cup blanched whole almonds or**
  1⅓ cups slivered almonds (5½ ounces)
- 4 **cups sifted powdered sugar**
- 2 **tablespoons water**
- 1 **tablespoon light-colored corn syrup**
- 1 **teaspoon almond extract**
- **Paste food coloring (optional)**

1. In a food processor, combine almonds and *1⅓ cups* of the powdered sugar. Cover and process until very finely ground. Add the water, corn syrup, and almond extract; cover and process until combined. Transfer to a large bowl. Stir in *1¼ cups* of the powdered sugar until combined.

2. Sprinkle a work surface with powdered sugar. Turn out almond mixture onto sugared surface; knead in *1 cup* of the powdered sugar until mixture is smooth.

3. If desired, divide marzipan; tint with food coloring. Mold or shape as desired, using about about *2 teaspoons* marzipan for each shape and additional powdered sugar as needed. To prevent sticking, coat hands lightly with powdered sugar. If attaching pieces (as for the pig pictured below), brush pieces with corn syrup. Makes about 2 cups mixture (1¼ pounds).

Children in Europe love marzipan, especially when it's shaped it into fanciful holiday figures, such as animals and fruits. In Denmark, the candy plays a special role—the diner who finds the single whole almond hidden inside the Christmas rice pudding (see recipe, page 106) wins a tiny marzipan pig!

Almond Paste Candy

Nutmeg-Apple Conserve
Prep: 45 minutes Process: 5 minutes

5	cups chopped, peeled apples
1	cup water
⅓	cup lemon juice
4	cups sugar
1	cup golden raisins
1	1¾-ounce package regular powdered fruit pectin
½	teaspoon ground nutmeg

Nutmeg-Apple Conserve

Jams, jellies, and other home-processed treasures from summer's rich harvest have been a welcome gift since the old days, when fresh fruit was a scarce and dear commodity. Old-world cooks spent weeks each summer "puttin' up" the fruits of their orchards and woodlands. Brimming jars were stashed away in cellars to be shared at holiday time and throughout the long winter. Although fruits and preserves today are more plentiful, one-of-a-kind jellies, conserves, and fruits processed in your kitchen still make endearing gifts. Even better, you can make them ahead and store in a cool, dark place for up to six months.

1. In a 6- or 8-quart Dutch oven, combine apples, water, and lemon juice. Bring to boiling; reduce heat. Cover and simmer for 10 minutes.

2. Stir in sugar and raisins. Cook and stir over medium heat until the sugar is dissolved. Bring to a full rolling boil, stirring constantly.

3. Stir in pectin; return to a full rolling boil, stirring constantly. Boil for 1 minute, stirring constantly. Remove from heat; stir in nutmeg.

4. Ladle hot mixture into six hot, sterilized ½-pint canning jars, leaving a ¼-inch headspace. Wipe jar rims; adjust lids. Process filled jars in a boiling-water canner for 5 minutes (start timing when water returns to boil). Remove jars; cool on a wire rack. Makes 6 (½-pint) gifts.

Lemon-Honey Jelly
Pictured on page 133.
Prep: 45 minutes Process: 5 minutes

2	to 3 medium lemons
1½	cups water
3½	cups sugar
¾	cup honey
½	of a 6-ounce package (1 foil pouch) liquid fruit pectin

1. Using a vegetable peeler, remove and reserve the yellow portion of the peel from *one* of the lemons. Squeeze enough of the lemons to get ½ cup juice.

2. In a 5- to 6-quart Dutch oven, combine lemon peel strips, the ½ cup lemon juice, and the water. Stir in sugar. Cook and stir over medium heat until the sugar is dissolved. Stir in honey. Bring to a full rolling boil (a boil that cannot be stirred down), stirring constantly.

3. Stir in the pectin; return to a full rolling boil. Boil for 1 minute, stirring constantly. Remove from heat. Use a metal spoon to quickly skim off the foam. Remove the lemon peel.

4. Ladle hot mixture into five hot, sterilized ½-pint canning jars, leaving a ¼-inch headspace. Wipe jar rims; adjust lids. Process filled jars in a boiling-water canner for 5 minutes (start timing when water returns to boil). Remove jars; cool on a wire rack. Makes 5 (½-pint) gifts.

Brandied Honey-and-Spice Pears
Prep: 35 minutes Process: 20 minutes

  6   **pounds pears (about 15 pears)**
Ascorbic acid color keeper*
  4   **cups cranberry juice, apple juice, or apple cider**
1½ **cups honey**
  ½   **cup lemon juice**
  3   **tablespoons chopped candied ginger**
  8   **inches stick cinnamon, broken into 2-inch pieces**
  ½   **teaspoon whole cloves**
  ¼   **cup brandy**

1. Wash, peel, halve, and core pears; place in ascorbic acid color-keeper solution as soon as peeled or cut.

2. In a 6- to 8-quart Dutch oven, combine cranberry juice, honey, lemon juice, ginger, cinnamon, and cloves. Bring to boiling. Add pears and brandy. Return to boiling; reduce heat. Simmer, uncovered, about 5 minutes or until pears are almost tender, stirring occasionally.

3. Pack hot pears into six hot, sterilized 1-pint canning jars, leaving ½-inch headspace. Cover with hot syrup, leaving ½-inch headspace. Remove any air bubbles. Wipe jar rims; adjust lids. Process filled jars in a boiling-water canner for 20 minutes (start timing when water returns to boil). Remove jars; cool on a wire rack. Makes 6 (1-pint) gifts.

*Note: To prevent cut pears from darkening, treat with ascorbic acid color keeper. Look for it in the produce or canning supply sections in the supermarket and follow the package directions.

139

Mint 'n' Cream Coffee Mix

Chocolate-Dipped Orange Peel

Prep: 2 hours   Cook: 2¼ hours
Dry: several hours   Chill: 20 minutes

- 4   large oranges
- 1½ cups sugar
- ¾ cup water
- 3   tablespoons light-colored corn syrup
- 4   ounces semisweet or bittersweet
  chocolate
- 1   tablespoon shortening

1. Score peel of each orange lengthwise into four sections. Using the bowl of a spoon, loosen orange peel from pulp; save oranges for another use. Place peel in a large saucepan; add enough water to cover. Bring to boiling; reduce heat. Cover; simmer for 20 minutes. Drain well. Repeat cooking and draining twice. Cool slightly.

2. Using a spoon, carefully scrape excess pulp from the peel. Cut peel into ¼-inch-wide strips.

3. For syrup, in a heavy, 2-quart saucepan, combine sugar, the ¾ cup water, and the corn syrup. Cook and stir over medium heat until mixture boils and sugar is dissolved.

4. Clip a candy thermometer to the side of the pan. Reduce heat to medium; continue cooking, without stirring, until the thermometer registers to 234°F to 240°F, soft-ball stage (about 40 minutes). (Adjust heat as necessary to maintain a steady boil.)

5. Remove thermometer. Add orange peel; simmer for 30 to 35 minutes or until peel is translucent, stirring frequently. Remove peel from syrup; drain well. Discard syrup. Dry peel on a wire rack for several hours.

6. Line a tray with waxed paper; set aside. In a small saucepan, combine chocolate and shortening; heat over low heat until melted, stirring often. Transfer to a small bowl.

7. Dip one end of each peel strip into the melted chocolate; drain off excess chocolate. Arrange on prepared tray. Chill in the refrigerator until chocolate is set. Makes 4 (½-cup) gifts.

Make-Ahead Tip: Prepare Chocolate-Dipped Orange Peel as directed. In an airtight container, layer orange peel between sheets of waxed paper; cover. Store in the refrigerator for up to 2 weeks.

Mint 'n' Cream Coffee Mix
Café au Lait (ka-fay oh LAY)
Start to finish: 10 minutes

- 2   cups nonfat dry milk powder
- ½   cup powdered nondairy creamer
- ½   cup butter mints, slightly crushed
- ¼   cup sifted powdered sugar
- ⅔   cup instant coffee crystals
- Peppermint sticks or striped round
  peppermint candies

1. In a medium bowl, stir together milk powder, creamer, mints, and sugar. In four 1-cup jars or mugs, layer mint mixture and coffee crystals. Insert peppermint candies as necessary to fill. Makes 4 (1-cup) gifts (16 servings).

To make Mint 'n' Cream Coffee: For each serving, place ¼ cup dry mix in a heat-proof mug; add ⅔ cup boiling water. Stir until dissolved. If desired, serve with a peppermint stick.

Make-Ahead Tip: Prepare Mint 'n' Cream Coffee Mix as directed; cover and store at room temperature for up to 1 month.

Thyme-and-Orange Vinegar

Pictured on page 133.
Prep: 30 minutes Cool: 3 hours
Stand: 2 weeks

- 1 medium orange
- 8 cups white wine vinegar
- 1 750-milliliter bottle dry white wine
    (3¼ cups)
- ½ cup packed fresh thyme sprigs
- Fresh thyme sprigs, rinsed and dried
    (optional)

1. Using a vegetable peeler, remove narrow strips of the orange portion of orange peel. (Squeeze orange and reserve juice for another purpose.) Set peel aside.

2. In a large stainless-steel, enamel, or nonstick kettle, combine vinegar, wine, the ½ cup thyme, and orange peel strips. Bring vinegar mixture almost to boiling; remove from heat. Cover kettle loosely with 100-percent-cotton cheesecloth; cool about 3 hours or until room temperature.

3. Pour vinegar mixture into a clean 1-gallon jar. Cover tightly with nonmetallic lid (or cover with plastic wrap and tightly seal with metal lid). Let stand in a cool, dark place for 2 weeks.

4. Line a colander with several layers of 100-percent-cotton cheesecloth or coffee filters; place over a large bowl. Pour vinegar mixture through colander into bowl. Discard solids.

5. Pour strained vinegar into clean ½-pint or larger jars or bottles. If desired, add a sprig of thyme to each. Cover with nonmetallic lids (or cover with plastic wrap and tightly seal with metal lids). Makes 6 (½-pint) gifts.

Pomegranate Vinegar: Prepare Thyme-and-Orange Vinegar as directed, except omit the thyme and add 1¼ cups pomegranate seeds. (To separate seeds from pomegranate, quarter 2 pomegranates. Fold peel back to expose seeds; remove seeds, discarding membrane and peel.) Place seeds in the large stainless-steel, enamel, or nonstick kettle; press seeds lightly with a potato masher to release the juices. Add vinegar, wine, and orange peel strips. Continue as directed. If desired, add a few additional pomegranate seeds to each jar or bottle.

Make-Ahead Tip: Prepare vinegar as directed. Store in a cool, dark place for up to 6 months.

Spiced Honey Butter

Start to finish: 5 minutes

- 2 cups butter or margarine, softened
- 1 cup honey
- 2 teaspoons ground cinnamon

1. In a medium bowl, combine butter, honey, and cinnamon; beat with an electric mixer on medium speed until light and fluffy. Spoon into three clean 1-cup jars; cover tightly. Cover and refrigerate until serving time. To serve, bring to room temperature. Makes 3 (1-cup) gifts.

Make-Ahead Tip: Prepare Spiced Honey Butter as directed. Cover and store in the refrigerator up to 1 week. Serve as directed.

Cranberry Vodka

Pictured on page 133.
Prep: 10 minutes Stand: 2 weeks

- 4 cups fresh or frozen cranberries
- 4 cups vodka

1. Wash cranberries; pat dry. Divide cranberries among four clean 1-pint jars. Pour 1 cup of the vodka over the fruit in each jar. Cover tightly with a nonmetallic lids (or cover jars with plastic wrap and tightly seal with metal lids). Let stand in a cool, dark place for 2 weeks. Makes 4 (1-pint) gifts.

Make-Ahead Tip: Prepare Cranberry Vodka as directed. Store in a cool, dark place for up to 2 months.

Until recently, vodka was prized for its clear, flavorless quality. Today, it's infused with all sorts of intriguing flavors and stars in strikingly creative martinis. Traditionalists needn't worry that flavored vodka is too "newfangled." Eastern Europeans have long infused their beloved vodka with flavorings, such as peppercorns, honey, and fruits. Cranberries, once known to early Americans as "bounce berries" (because they bounce when ripe), add jolly American holiday appeal to the spirit.

Spinach-Stuffed Chicken in Phyllo
Kotopita (koh-toh-PEE-tah)
Prep: 1 hour Bake: 30 minutes

1	large onion, chopped (1 cup)
1	tablespoon olive oil or cooking oil
4	cups loosely packed fresh baby spinach
½	of an 8-ounce package cream cheese, softened and cubed
1	tablespoon all-purpose flour
1	teaspoon dried rosemary, crushed
½	teaspoon ground nutmeg
1	egg yolk
4	ounces mozzarella cheese, shredded
4	ounces feta cheese, crumbled (1 cup)
8	skinless, boneless chicken breast halves (about 2½ pounds total)

Salt

Ground black pepper

24	sheets frozen phyllo dough (14x9-inch rectangles), thawed
⅔	cup butter or margarine, melted
1	recipe Rosemary-Mushroom Sauce (opposite)

1. For filling, in a large skillet, cook onion in hot oil until tender. Stir in spinach; cook and stir until wilted. Remove from heat. Add cream cheese; stir until mixed. Stir in flour, rosemary, and nutmeg. Beat egg yolk; stir into spinach mixture. Stir in mozzarella and feta cheeses.

2. Meanwhile, place each chicken breast half between two sheets of plastic wrap. Using the flat side of a meat mallet, pound to ⅛-inch thickness; remove wrap. Sprinkle with salt and pepper. Place about ¼ *cup* of the filling on each chicken piece; roll each into a spiral (do not seal ends). Preheat oven to 350°F.

3. Unroll phyllo dough; cover with plastic wrap to prevent drying. Place *one* phyllo sheet on a flat work surface; brush with melted butter. Top with *two* more sheets, brushing each with butter.

4. Place a chicken roll near the short side of the buttered phyllo stack; roll chicken and phyllo once to cover chicken. Fold in long sides; continue rolling from short side. Place in a shallow baking pan. Repeat with remaining chicken rolls, phyllo, and butter. Brush with any remaining butter.

Spinach-Stuffed Chicken in Phyllo

For a memorable entrée at your New Year's dinner party, take your inspiration from Greece. This phyllo-wrapped chicken is reminiscent of a Greek chicken pie known as *Kotopita*. And while you're opening your home to guests on New Year's Eve, be sure to note who crosses your threshold first. According to Greek folklore, they will bring your family good luck in the coming year.

5. Bake phyllo rolls, uncovered, for 30 to 35 minutes or until chicken is no longer pink (170°F). Serve with Rosemary-Mushroom Sauce. Makes 8 servings.

Rosemary-Mushroom Sauce: In a medium saucepan, melt ¼ cup butter or margarine over medium heat. Add 2 cups sliced fresh mushrooms (button or crimini) and 2 cloves garlic, minced. Cook and stir until tender. Stir in 2 tablespoons all-purpose flour; 1 teaspoon dried rosemary, crushed; ¼ teaspoon salt; and ¼ teaspoon ground black pepper. Add 1½ cups milk all at once. Cook and stir until thickened and bubbly. Cook and stir for 2 minutes more. Stir in ¼ cup dry white wine or additional milk.

Make-Ahead Tip: Prepare Spinach-Stuffed Chicken in Phyllo as directed through step 2. Cover; chill in the refrigerator for up to 8 hours. Wrap chicken rolls in phyllo; bake as directed in steps 3 through 5.

Honey-Dipped Cookies
Melamakárona (mel-ah-mah-KAR-rone ah)
Prep: 30 minutes Bake: 13 minutes per batch

½	cup butter, softened
⅓	cup cooking oil
⅓	cup sugar
1	tablespoon orange juice
1	teaspoon baking powder
½	teaspoon baking soda
¼	teaspoon ground cloves
2	cups all-purpose flour
	Whole cloves (optional)*
¾	cup sugar
½	cup water
⅓	cup honey
⅓	cup finely chopped walnuts, toasted

1. In a large bowl, beat butter with an electric mixer on medium to high speed for 30 seconds. Beat in oil. Add the ⅓ cup sugar; beat until combined, scraping side of bowl occasionally. Add orange juice, baking powder, baking soda, and ground cloves; beat well. Beat in flour. Preheat oven to 350°F.

2. Shape dough into 1¼-inch balls. Arrange balls 1 inch apart on ungreased cookie sheet. If desired, push a clove into the top of each cookie.

3. Bake for 13 to 15 minutes or until bottoms are light brown. Remove from cookie sheet; cool on a wire rack.

4. For syrup, in a small saucepan, combine the ¾ cup sugar, the water, and honey. Bring to boiling; reduce heat. Simmer, uncovered, for 5 minutes. Dip cooled cookies into warm syrup. Sprinkle immediately with nuts. Let dry on a wire rack. Makes about 24 cookies.

Make-Ahead Tip: Prepare Honey-Dipped Cookies as directed. In an airtight container, arrange dipped cookies in layers between sheets of waxed paper; cover. Store at room temperature for up to 2 days. (Or place undipped cookies in a freezer container; freeze for up to 1 month. Thaw cookies. Prepare syrup; dip cookies as directed.)

***Note:** The whole cloves are a traditional decoration in these cookies, but remove them before eating the buttery rounds.

Bishop
Bisschop (biz-SHUP)
Pictured on page 142.
Prep: 10 minutes Cook: 30 minutes

6	inches stick cinnamon, broken
1	teaspoon whole cloves
1	medium orange, sliced
1	medium lemon, sliced
1	cup sugar
1	cup water
2	750-milliliter bottles dry red wine
	Stick cinnamon (optional)

1. For spice bag, place the 6 inches stick cinnamon and the whole cloves in center of a double-thick, 6-inch square of 100-percent-cotton cheesecloth. Bring corners of cheesecloth together; tie with clean kitchen string.

2. In a Dutch oven, combine spice bag, sliced orange, sliced lemon, sugar, and water. Bring to boiling, stirring to dissolve sugar. Reduce heat to medium-low. Add wine. Heat, uncovered, for 30 minutes (do not boil).

3. Remove spice bag and citrus slices. Pour into a heat-proof punch bowl. If desired, garnish each serving with additional stick cinnamon. Makes about 10 (6-ounce) servings.

St. Basil's Bread

St. Basil's Bread
Vaslopita (vahz-loh-PEE-tuh)
Prep: 30 minutes Rise: 1½ hours
Bake: 20 minutes

4	to 4½ cups all-purpose flour
1	package active dry yeast
1	teaspoon finely shredded lemon peel
½	teaspoon anise seeds, crushed
1	cup milk
¼	cup butter
¼	cup sugar
¾	teaspoon salt
2	eggs
1	egg yolk
1	tablespoon water
Sesame seeds	

1. In a large bowl, stir together *2 cups* of the flour, yeast, lemon peel, and anise seeds; set aside.

2. In a small saucepan, heat and stir milk, butter, sugar, and salt just until warm (120°F to 130°F) and butter is almost melted. Add to flour mixture. Add eggs. Beat with an electric mixer on low for 30 seconds. Beat on high for 3 minutes, scraping bowl constantly. Using a wooden spoon, stir in as much of the remaining flour as you can.

3. Turn out dough onto a lightly floured surface. Knead in enough of the remaining flour to make a moderately stiff dough that is smooth and elastic (6 to 8 minutes total). Shape dough into a ball. Place in a lightly greased bowl; turn once to grease the surface. Cover; let rise in a warm place until double in size (1 to 1¼ hours).

4. Punch down dough. Turn out onto a lightly floured surface. Divide into thirds. Cover; let rest for 10 minutes. Meanwhile, grease two 8×1½-inch round baking pans; set aside.

5. Shape two dough portions into flat 8-inch round loaves; place in prepared baking pans. Divide remaining dough in half. Shape each half into a 20-inch-long rope; twist and seal ends to form two 7-inch circles. Place a circle on each loaf. In a small bowl, beat egg yolk and the water; brush onto loaves. Sprinkle with sesame seeds. Cover; let rise in a warm place until nearly double in size (30 to 45 minutes). Preheat oven to 375°F.

6. Bake 20 to 25 minutes or until it sounds hollow. If necessary, cover loosely with foil for the last 5 minutes of baking. Remove from pans; cool on wire racks. Makes 2 loaves (16 servings).

On January 1, Greeks celebrate St. Basil's Day. A forefather of the Greek Orthodox Church, St. Basil was known for his generosity to the poor. When this bread is served, one slice is reserved for the good saint, a second for the poor, and a third is offered to the eldest member of the family. Traditionally, a coin is baked inside the loaf, and the one who finds it will be lucky all year.

King's Bread Ring

Prep: 30 minutes Rise: 2¾ hours
Bake: 35 minutes

  3 to 3½ cups all-purpose flour
  1 package active dry yeast
  ⅔ cup milk
  ⅔ cup butter
  ⅔ cup sugar
  1 teaspoon salt
  2 eggs
  ½ teaspoon ground cinnamon
  ⅔ cup diced mixed candied fruits and peels
  ¾ cup chopped Brazil nuts or almonds

1. In a large bowl, stir together *1½ cups* of the flour and the yeast; set aside.

2. In a small saucepan, heat and stir milk, *6 tablespoons* of the butter, *⅓ cup* of the sugar, and the salt just until warm (120°F to 130°F) and butter is almost melted. Add to flour mixture. Add eggs. Beat with an electric mixer on low speed for 30 seconds. Beat on high speed for 3 minutes, scraping bowl. Using a wooden spoon, stir in as much of the remaining flour as you can.

3. Turn out dough onto a lightly floured surface. Knead in enough remaining flour to make a moderately stiff dough that is smooth and elastic (6 to 8 minutes total). Shape into a ball. Place in a greased bowl; turn once. Cover; let rise in a warm place until double (1¾ to 2 hours).

4. Punch down dough. Turn out onto a lightly floured surface. Cover; let rest for 10 minutes. Meanwhile, grease a baking sheet; set aside.

5. Roll dough to a 24×12-inch rectangle. Brush with *2 tablespoons* of melted butter. In a small bowl, stir together *2 tablespoons* of the sugar and the cinnamon; sprinkle onto dough. In a small bowl, combine candied fruits and peels and *½ cup* of the nuts; sprinkle onto dough. Starting from a long side, roll up into a spiral; seal seams.

6. On prepared baking sheet, shape roll into a ring. Cover; let rise in a warm place until nearly double in size (about 1 hour).

7. Bake in a 325°F oven for 35 to 40 minutes or until golden. If necessary, cover loosely with foil for the last 5 minutes. Remove bread from baking sheet. Cool on a wire rack. Brush with remaining melted butter; sprinkle with remaining nuts and sugar. Makes 1 ring (12 servings).

Sweet Cross Bread

Massa Sovada (mahz-ah soh-VAH-dah)
Prep: 30 minutes Rise: 2½ hours
Bake: 50 minutes

  4 to 4½ cups all-purpose flour
  2 packages active dry yeast
  1 cup milk
  ⅔ cup sugar
  6 tablespoons butter
  ½ teaspoon salt
  2 eggs
  1 egg white

1. In a large bowl, combine *1½ cups* of the flour and the yeast; set aside.

2. In a small saucepan, heat and stir milk, sugar, butter, and salt just until warm (120°F to 130°F) and butter is almost melted, stirring occasionally. Add to flour mixture. Add the two eggs. Beat with an electric mixer on low speed for 30 seconds. Beat for 3 minutes on high speed, scraping the side of the bowl constantly. Using a wooden spoon, stir in as much of the remaining flour as you can.

3. Turn out dough onto a lightly floured surface. Knead in enough of the remaining flour to make a moderately stiff dough that is smooth and elastic (6 to 8 minutes total). Shape into a ball. Place in a lightly greased bowl; turn once to grease the surface. Cover; let rise in warm place until nearly double in size (about 2 hours).

4. Punch down dough. Turn out onto a lightly floured surface. Cover; let rest for 10 minutes. Meanwhile, grease a large baking sheet; set aside.

5. Shape dough into a ball. Place on prepared baking sheet. Pat or roll to an 8-inch round. Cover; let rise in a warm place until nearly double in size (30 to 45 minutes). Preheat oven to 325°F.

6. Using a sharp knife, cut an "X" on top of the loaf. Beat egg white; brush onto dough. Bake for 20 minutes.

7. Cover loosely with foil to prevent overbrowning. Bake for 30 to 40 minutes more or until loaf sounds hollow when tapped. Remove from baking sheet. Cool on a wire rack. Makes 1 loaf (20 servings).

Black Bun

Prep: 45 minutes Bake: 1¾ hours
Cool: 45 minutes Chill: 8 hours

- 1   cup golden raisins
- 1   cup dried currants
- ½   cup diced mixed candied fruits and peels
- 1   recipe Pastry for a Double-Crust Pie (below right)
- 1½ cups all-purpose flour
- ½   cup packed brown sugar
- 1   teaspoon baking soda
- 1   teaspoon cream of tartar
- 1   teaspoon ground cinnamon
- 1   teaspoon ground ginger
- 1   egg
- ⅔   cup milk
- ½   cup Scotch whisky
- 2   tablespoons butter, melted
- ½   cup chopped almonds

Milk

Granulated sugar

Black Bun

1. In a medium bowl, combine raisins, currants, and candied fruits and peels; cover with boiling water. Let stand for 10 minutes.

2. Meanwhile, on a lightly floured surface, roll *two-thirds* of the Pastry for a Double-Crust Pie to a 13-inch round. Transfer pastry to an ungreased 8-inch springform pan; ease pastry into pan, lining bottom and side. Trim pastry to extend ¾ inch beyond edge of pan.

3. For filling, in a large bowl, stir together flour, brown sugar, baking soda, cream of tartar, cinnamon, and ginger. In a small bowl, beat egg; stir in the ⅔ cup milk, whisky, and butter. Add to flour mixture, stirring until smooth. Drain fruit; fold fruit and almonds into egg mixture.

4. Spoon filling into pastry. Roll out remaining pastry to an 8-inch round. Place on filling. Brush edge with water. Fold bottom pastry over top pastry; crimp to seal. Using a fork, prick top crust; brush with milk. Cut out decorative pieces from pastry trimmings; arrange on crust. Brush with milk; sprinkle with granulated sugar.

5. Bake in a 300°F oven for 1¾ hours. Cool in the pan on a wire rack for 15 minutes. Using a sharp knife, loosen crust from the side of the pan; cool for 30 minutes more.

6. Remove the side of the pan; cool on a wire rack. Wrap in plastic wrap or foil. Chill for 8 hours to 1 week. Makes 12 to 16 servings.

Pastry for a Double-Crust Pie: In a medium bowl, stir together 2 cups all-purpose flour and 1 teaspoon salt. Using a pastry blender, cut in ⅔ cup shortening until pieces are pea-size. Sprinkle 1 tablespoon cold water over part of the flour mixture; gently toss with a fork. Push moistened dough to the side of the bowl. Repeat with an additional 5 to 6 tablespoons cold water, using 1 tablespoon water at a time, until all flour mixture is moistened. Form into a ball.

Hogmanay is what the Scots call New Year's Eve, and the cities of Edinburgh and Glasgow light up with exuberant street parties, torchlight processions, fireworks, and—at midnight—plenty of kissing and rounds of "Auld Lang Syne." On *Hogmanay,* it's considered good luck if, at the strike of midnight, a tall, dark stranger crosses your doorstep. Of course, you must offer him drink and lucky food, including *Black Bun,* a dark fruit cake dressed in a flaky, golden crust.

Known as *Galette des Rois*—or Cake of Kings—this almond pastry is served in France on Epiphany (the Twelfth Night) to commemorate the visit of the Three Kings. Traditionally, a bean or token is baked into the cake. Whoever finds the bean in his (or her) slice is either designated king (or queen) for the day or ls assured to have good luck in the coming year. Rather than wearing a traditional paper crown, this version is topped with a mixture of candied fruits, tossed with a spoonful of honey.

King's Almond Pastry Tart

King's Almond Pastry Tart
Galette des Rois (gah-LEHT day roy)
Prep: 30 minutes Chill: 2 hours
Bake: 23 minutes

½ cup slivered almonds
½ cup sifted powdered sugar
¼ cup butter, cut up
1 tablespoon all-purpose flour
2 eggs
1 17.3-ounce package (2 sheets) frozen puff pastry
1 tablespoon milk
2 tablespoons light-colored corn syrup

1. In a food processor, combine almonds and *1 tablespoon* powdered sugar. Cover and process until almonds are ground but not buttery. Add remaining sugar, butter, and flour. Cover; process until combined. Add *one* egg. Cover; process until mixed. Cover; chill for 1 hour.

2. Meanwhile, let folded puff pastry thaw at room temperature for 30 minutes. Line a baking sheet with parchment paper; set aside.

3. Unfold pastry. From each pastry sheet, cut out a 9-inch round. Place a round on the prepared baking sheet. Spread chilled almond mixture to within 2 inches of edge of pastry.

4. In a small bowl, use a fork to beat together remaining egg and milk; brush onto edge of pastry. Top with the remaining puff pastry round. Press edges together to seal.

5. If desired, using a scalloped pastry cutter or a sharp knife, cut edge of pastry to form a scalloped edge. (Remove and discard excess pastry.) To score a pattern in the top, start in the center and make a shallow cut in a slightly curved spokelike fashion to the edge of the pastry (not through the pastry). Cover; chill for 1 to 2 hours. Preheat oven to 400°F.

6. Bake for 15 minutes. In a small bowl, combine corn syrup and the water; brush onto partially baked pastry. Bake about 8 minutes more or until golden.

7. Carefully remove pastry from baking sheet; cool on a wire rack. If desired, sprinkle with additional powdered sugar; top with fruit, if desired. Makes 8 servings.

Fairy Tale Cottage

ONCE UPON A TIME, deep in the Black Forest of Germany, a tale was told of a house good enough to eat. The Grimm Brothers' story of *Hansel and Gretel*, about a witch's hut made of cookies, candies, and icing, is beloved to children around the world. That simple tale has inspired German and other cooks to bake fanciful houses for the holidays. This two-tone, two-room gingerbread house looks much like the one Hansel and Gretel found in the story so long ago, only it uses readymade cookies and candies for easy decorating. Try putting it together with your family this holiday, and see if you all live happily ever after!

Fairy Tale Cottage (directions begin on page 152)

Gingerbread Cookie Dough
Prep: 15 minutes Chill: 3 hours

½ cup butter
½ cup shortening
1 cup sugar
1½ teaspoons ground ginger
1½ teaspoons ground allspice
1 teaspoon baking soda
½ teaspoon salt
1 egg
½ cup molasses
2 tablespoons lemon juice
3 cups all-purpose flour
1 cup whole wheat flour

1. In a large bowl, beat butter and shortening with electric mixer on medium to high speed for 30 seconds. Add sugar, ginger, allspice, baking soda, and salt; beat until combined. Add egg, molasses, and lemon juice; beat until combined.

2. Beat in as much of the all-purpose flour as you can with the mixer. Using a wooden spoon, stir in any remaining all-purpose flour and the whole wheat flour. Divide dough in half. Wrap each half in plastic wrap. Chill about 3 hours or until firm enough to handle.

Note: Make two batches of gingerbread dough.

Sugar Cookie Dough
Prep: 15 minutes Chill: 2 hours

1½ cups butter
2 cups sugar
¼ teaspoon baking soda
1 egg
4 cups all-purpose flour

1. In a large bowl, beat butter with electric mixer on medium to high speed for 30 seconds. Add sugar and baking soda; beat until combined. Add egg; beat until combined.

2. Beat in as much of the flour as you can with the mixer. Using a wooden spoon, stir in any remaining flour. Divide dough into four portions. Wrap each portion in plastic wrap. Chill dough about 2 hours or until firm enough to handle.

Royal Icing
Start to finish: 15 minutes

4½ cups sifted powdered sugar
3 tablespoons meringue powder
½ teaspoon cream of tartar
½ cup warm water
1 teaspoon vanilla

1. In a medium bowl, stir together powdered sugar, meringue powder, and cream of tartar. Add warm water and vanilla.

2. Beat with an electric mixer on high speed for 7 to 10 minutes or until very stiff. Cover with plastic wrap; chill for up to 24 hours. Beat with an electric mixer until stiff. Makes 3 cups.

Note: Make two batches of icing.

Materials
2 recipes Gingerbread Cookie Dough
1 recipe Sugar Cookie Dough
2 recipes Royal Icing
Paper pattern (opposite)
Paste food coloring
Decorating bag and tips
Wafer-creme cookies, separated into layers
Fruit-flavored circle candies
Tiny flavor-coated gum
Graham cracker squares
Multicolored nonpareils
Peanut halves
Frosted bite-size shredded wheat biscuits
Candy sticks
Gumdrops
Quilt batting
Gingersnaps
Mixed nuts
Pretzel sticks
Sugar and waffle ice cream cones
Small silver and gold decorative candies

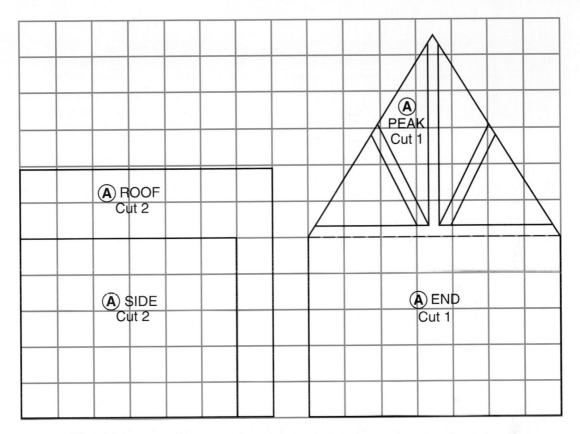

Use these patterns to cut out the dough pieces for the Fairy Tale Cottage. To enlarge the patterns, redraw them so each square equals an inch. Or enlarge them on a copy machine by 400 percent.

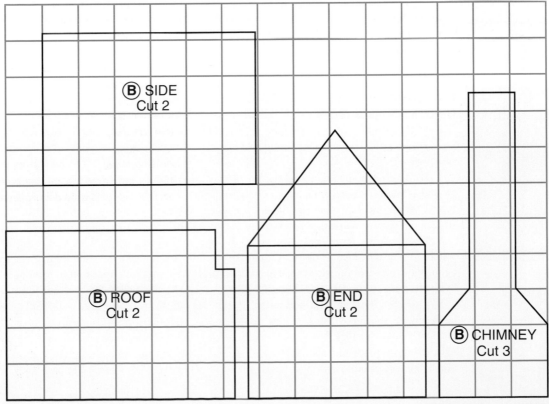

1 SQUARE = 1 INCH

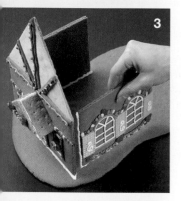

Cutting and Baking

1. Prepare doughs (page 152). Enlarge and cut out patterns. Use one portion dough at a time; keep remaining chilled. Preheat oven to 375°F.

2. On the back of an ungreased 15x10x1-inch baking pan, using a floured rolling pin, roll out Sugar Cookie Dough to ¼-inch thickness. Cut two roof patterns A. Cut two roof patterns B (see photo 1), reversing pattern for second piece. Roll out trimmings; cut one peak pattern A.

3. Line an extra-large baking sheet with foil. On foil, roll out a portion of Gingerbread Cookie Dough to a 16½×12-inch rectangle; trim.

4. On lightly floured surface, roll out remaining gingerbread dough to ¼-inch thickness. Cut out two each side patterns A, end patterns A, side patterns B, and end patterns B. Cut three chimney patterns. Using dough scraps, cut out four ¼-inch-wide strips.

5. On a baking sheet, position end section A and peak section A with long edges touching. Roll lightly to seal. Place four ¼-inch-wide strips on peak to form beams (see photo 2).

6. Bake pieces, in batches, for 10 to 12 minutes or until edges are light brown. While warm, place paper patterns on cookie pieces; trim dough. Cool slightly. Transfer to wire racks; cool.

Decorating

1. Prepare Royal Icing (page 152). Leaving at least three-quarters of the icing white, use paste food coloring to tint portions green, red, yellow, and other desired colors. Fill pastry or decorating bags (fitted with couplers, if desired) with icings. Cover; store remaining icing in the refrigerator.

2. Using white icing and medium round tip, pipe windows and doors onto side and end pieces (see photo 2).

3. Using green icing and round tip, pipe a line around windows and doors. Pipe light strings onto beams. With medium star tip, pipe evergreen swag under each window (see photo, page 150).

4. Using white icing and same tip, attach wafers for shutters; pipe scroll onto each. Attach circle candy wreaths on windows. Trim with gum pieces (see photos 3 and page 150).

5. Using red icing and medium round tip, pipe bows under shutters. Using yellow icing and medium round tip, pipe bows onto wreaths. For light strings, pipe dabs of red, green, yellow, and blue icing (see photo, page 150). Let dry.

Assembling

1. For porch, break graham cracker squares in half to form two rectangles; cut another square in half diagonally to form two triangles. Trim one triangle with green icing swag and red icing bow; sprinkle swag with nonpareils (discard remaining triangle). Assemble porch roof (see photo, page 150), attaching pieces with white icing.

2. For cottage walls, use coffee mugs or glass tumblers to hold pieces in place. Using a decorating bag fitted with a coupler and medium round tip, pipe white icing lines along bottom edge of two-toned end section A and bottom and side edges of each side section B. Position two-toned end section A near end of cookie base. Position a side section B at each end of end section A (see photo 3). Hold in place with mugs. Position end sections B and side sections A (see photo 4), gluing in place with icing. Let dry.

3. For roofs, using round tip, pipe white icing onto top edges of side and end pieces. Press roof pieces into position, placing notched ends of roof sections B at the outside edge (see photo 4).

4. For chimney, stack three chimney pieces together; glue with white icing. Use icing to attach chimney to end of cottage section B, fitting into notched area of roof. Spread a small area of chimney with white icing. Place peanut halves on icing (see photo 5). Repeat until chimney is covered with icing and nuts. Let dry.

5. For thatch, starting at the peak of the roof, spread part of a roof section generously with white icing. Press frosted bite-size shredded wheat biscuits into icing, staggering the rows (see photo, page 150). Repeat until all roof sections are covered with icing and wheat squares.

6. For icicles, using a decorating bag filled with white icing and fitted with the medium star tip, touch tip to roof edge. Squeeze bag gently, tapering icing to a point; pull tip away. Repeat on all roof edges (see photo, page 150). Spread icing onto porch roof; add a few small icicles.

7. For porch pillars, use white icing to attach 2 candy sticks to 2 gumdrops. Attach candy sticks to bottom of porch roof to form pillars.

8. For house, set on a surface covered with quilt batting. Arrange walk, wall, woodpile, trees, and light post as desired, using gingersnaps, mixed nuts, pretzels, cones, nonpareils, candy sticks, circle candies, gumdrops, and silver and gold candies (see photo, page 150).

Recipe Index by Country

Note: Pages in italics refer to photographs when pictured on a different page from recipes.

A-B

Recipe Index

Recipe Index